PRAISE FOR

UNLIKELY AND ANOINTED

"God has an extraordinary way of choosing the most unexpected people in the most unlikely places to accomplish His purposes. In *Unlikely and Anointed,* Faith has masterfully crafted a road map that empowers every follower of Jesus to tap into the divine potential within them. This book is a clarion call to embrace the faith adventure that God has uniquely designed for each of us. Faith dismantles the misconceptions that hold us back—those lies that whisper we're not enough or that God can't use us. With clarity and boldness, she reminds us that God's power is alive and active in our lives, equipping us to step confidently into our world, ready to impact it for His glory."

—CHRISTINE CAINE,
founder of A21 and Propel Women

"We don't have a gifting problem; we have a belief problem. We've believed that power belongs to the few, when Jesus clearly gives it to all who believe—the unlikely and the ordinary. Faith tears down the lie that is stealing our power with both tenderness and authority, which she carries beautifully. I am grateful and excited to see the fruit of this book in the church and in your life."

—Zach Meerkreebs, DMin,
encourager, author, speaker, and pastor
in residence at Asbury University

"Some books inform. This one awakens. *Unlikely and Anointed* comes at exactly the right moment, when influencer culture has confused platform with power and following with anointing. Faith cuts through it all with warmth but conviction; her writing is as disarming as she is, with no pretense, no performance. The message is both ancient and urgent: The Holy Spirit doesn't anoint the most followed; He anoints the faithful, and every believer carries what the world is desperate for. I cannot wait to see what happens when readers actually believe that—thank you, Faith, for this gift."

—Becky Johnson, lead pastor of Jesus Culture Sacramento

BOOKS BY FAITH EURY CHO

NONFICTION

Experiencing Friendship with God

Deepen Your Friendship with God

CHILDREN'S

Never Alone

UNLIKELY AND ANOINTED

UNLIKELY AND ANOINTED

HOW EVERYDAY BELIEVERS EXPERIENCE THE POWER OF THE HOLY SPIRIT

FAITH EURY CHO

WATERBROOK

WaterBrook

An imprint of the Penguin Random House Christian Publishing Group,
a division of Penguin Random House LLC

1745 Broadway, New York, NY 10019

waterbrookmultnomah.com
penguinrandomhouse.com

Italics in Scripture quotations reflect the author's added emphasis.

A WaterBrook Trade Paperback Original

Trade Paperback ISBN 978-0-593-60302-4
Ebook ISBN 978-0-593-60303-1

The Cataloging-in-Publication Data is on file with the Library of Congress.

Printed in the United States of America

1st Printing

The authorized representative in the EU for product safety and compliance is Penguin Random House Ireland, Morrison Chambers, 32 Nassau Street, Dublin D02 YH68, Ireland.
https://eu-contact.penguin.ie

Book Team: Editor: Jamie Lapeyrolerie • Production editor: Laura Wright • Managing editor: Julia Wallace • Production manager: Mark Maguire • Copy editor: Lisa Grimenstein • Proofreaders: Tracey Moore, Aria Fischer

Adobe Stock Illustrations: Alexander Potapov (title page art), seliaz (dedication page art and chapter opening art), Thomas (part opening art)

Book design by Jo Anne Metsch

For details on special quantity discounts for bulk purchases, contact specialmarketscms@penguinrandomhouse.com.

To my parents, Kevin and MeeAe Kim.
Because of you, my life has been carried and
covered in prayer. Love you always.

CONTENTS

INTRODUCTION

You are a powerful Christian. You don't need to wait or work to become one because you already are one. The moment you believe that is the moment your journey of becoming an *impactful* Christian begins. Whether you are new in your relationship with Jesus or are a veteran of the faith, there's so much more to your walk with Him than what you've experienced so far. Life with our almighty and eternal God holds endless potential to intimately know the redeeming presence and power of the Holy Spirit.

As soon as you become a believer in Christ, you are a Christian with the capacity for a compelling compassion that touches even the most stubborn of hearts to consider eternity. A Christian with a contagious faith that shifts a room full of doubt into holy reverence. A Christian whose prayers shake nations and confound demonic principalities. A Christian who makes an eternal difference in someone else.

As you begin this journey with me today, you may not feel like a powerful Christian. I get it. I find that many do not. Perhaps it's because of the assumption that a powerful Christian is also a sensational one. You can probably picture someone like that in your head:

- the mic-holding, stage-striding faith speaker
- the charismatic role model with the viral testimony
- the faithful member everyone esteems at your church
- the astute Bible reader who has a thought-provoking answer to everything
- the angelic woman who lives the picture-perfect "happily married with kids" life

In other words, it may seem that a powerful Christian is someone who has that "I pray at 5 A.M. and go for a quick run every morning" sort of discipline to earn that impressive sparkle and shine. You might wonder if some people are inherently better at following God. *Maybe they love Jesus more than I do?* But therein lies the misconception. You cannot earn God's power with merit. You cannot become more deserving of it. On the contrary, you already carry it. This is why I wrote this book. I want to introduce you—or maybe reintroduce you—to true redeeming power: the anointing of the Holy Spirit. It's what enables us to become like Christ and to live in His power.

While I had been brewing on this message for a while, when it was time to finally put thoughts to paper, I was suddenly diagnosed with an onslaught of physical ailments—Lyme disease, mold intoxication, and hypothyroidism, just to name a few. The irony is that I was tasked to put down fifty thousand words about God's power in us while not even having the strength to lift my head off the pillow. My days were foggy, and my memory was glitchy. I was forgetting names and words that I use all the time, which is not fun for anyone, but especially for an author.

As the months passed, I became weaker, and discouragement

sank its talons into me. At one point, a script of hopelessness began rolling through my mind—maybe God's power wasn't with me at all. Perhaps my role in His kingdom was to sit on the sidelines and cheer on the real MVPs, the ones who were dedicated and gifted enough to stay in the game. Maybe if I had prayed more, this wouldn't have happened or, at least, I would have gotten better by now. I wondered if there was something inherently inept about my faith that disqualified me from being a worthy instrument of the Holy Spirit. These thoughts were very real for me. But I've discovered that even the most seasoned and experienced Christians may be hiding thoughts like these underneath their displays of faithfulness. Perhaps you can relate to some of them:

- Your prayers are only for blessing meals because the bold petitions to help the dying children in war-torn countries are for the "true prayer warriors" who pray all the time.
- Although you could encourage your co-workers with your own words, you prefer to send them a YouTube link to a sermon because the preacher there "says it better."
- You bring your sick family member to someone else for healing prayer, someone who seems closer to God.
- You keep the twenty-dollar bill in your wallet when asked to help those in need because you figure, *What's my twenty dollars to someone else's whopping thousand that's surely going toward the same cause?*
- When you hear tales of missionaries sacrificing their lives to preach the gospel in forbidden lands, you

applaud, smile, and nod while continuing to live your life as is because that sort of commission is for the "chosen ones" who have what it takes.

In John 14:12, Jesus said to His disciples, "Truly I tell you, the one who believes in me will also do the works that I do. And he will do even greater works than these, because I am going to the Father." I've heard this verse read aloud in churches countless times, with the congregation instinctively affirming it with an "Amen." Yet if you were to really unpack that amen, you might notice we're agreeing to something that God didn't mean! When we hear that we can be doing "greater works," we may think, *I really* can *get through this week!* or *I* will *get that job!* Now, don't get me wrong here. Coming to these convictions is not inherently wrong. God does bless in this way. However, if we are to be true to what Jesus meant, these are not the "greater works" He is talking about.

The Greek word for "works" in John 14:12 is the same one used in Matthew 11:2, when John the Baptist heard about the miracles and teachings that caused the people to stir while he was imprisoned. John sent his disciples to confirm what he was hearing: "Are you the one who is to come, or should we expect someone else?"* To strengthen John's faith, Jesus told John's disciples to return to him with a report of His works, the very works that we ourselves are called to do today. The report was, "The blind receive their sight, the lame walk, those with leprosy are cleansed, the deaf hear, the dead are raised, and the poor are told the good news."† This was the sort of kingdom activity

* Matthew 11:3.
† Matthew 11:5.

that Jesus was preparing the disciples for in John 14:12! They were to continue *His* works rather than accomplish an elevated version of their own interests and ambitions. Jesus spent the three years of His ministry performing miracles, casting out demons, healing the sick, teaching the truth, and changing lives. And now He was passing the baton. As if the bar wasn't high enough, Jesus said even *greater* works were to be done!

To clarify, who was chosen for these extraordinary works?

Those who believe and follow Jesus.

That's it. That's the condition.

This means that in a room of hundreds of believers at a church worship service, it isn't just the preacher and worship team on stage who are called to do the great works of Jesus. It isn't relegated to those who make church work their full-time job. It isn't just for the ordained Christian, the older Christian, or the picture-perfect Christian. Neither is it solely for those with millions of Instagram followers or a PhD. No, Jesus made it perfectly clear.

If you believe in Jesus, you are chosen to participate in His great works.

Yes, *you* are chosen.

Being educated and experienced is not a requirement for God's kingdom work. Being acknowledged and known by church leaders for your spiritual gifting is not always the mark of God's approval. Being married with kids is not the proof of maturity that merits you a significant role in our Father's business. Being knowledgeable and accomplished are not prerequisites to participate in redemptive history.

It's your faith that qualifies you, even if there's just a dribble of it. For years, I understood this on a cerebral level, but it became a burning conviction while writing this book. Because of the daily fatigue and compromised cognitive abilities, I asked the Lord if I should take time off from ministry to regain strength before continuing to work. I was painfully aware that I did not have what it takes. Even so, the only word I received from Him while in prayer was this: "Faith, you know your weaknesses very well, but you will now begin to understand My perfect power."

It is time to simultaneously raise and lower our expectations for Christians today. We must raise our expectations of what everyday Christians are meant to do. We are not bystanders who are destined to applaud the few superstars commissioned for the big plays. Nor are we meant to watch helplessly in the stands as the world is ravaged by darkness. Yet we must also lower our expectations of who we believe is meant to be an empowered vessel of the Holy Spirit. It is not always the most standout Christian you know. Have you ever watched any of the Marvel Avengers movies? Most people who watch these larger-than-life heroes on the big screen are drawn to one of the main characters. Maybe you want to be as rich and intelligent as Iron Man. Maybe you want to be as resilient and unstoppable as Black Widow. As a society, we are conditioned to connect with main characters and ignore the extras in the background. The guy that just ran out of his car to evade the alien attack in NYC is not a part of the plot. It's Hulk or Captain America. Do you see what I'm getting at?

But this is not how the kingdom of God works. God's activity on earth isn't centered on superhuman, larger-than-life characters. What makes any believer significant and special is the Holy Spirit in them. Each one of us—whether we are gas station attendants, platformed preachers, schoolteachers, baristas, students, stay-at-home parents, or business owners—has a significant role in God's Great Commission, and countless souls depend on it.

In this book, we're first going to dig beneath all our façades and layers to take an honest look at who we really are—flaws and all. The goal is not to get ourselves all depressed about where we fall short but, rather, to take a good look at the residence that the Holy Spirit has intentionally chosen to dwell in (you!). Then, we will unpack the power that's been given to us by the blood of Jesus and His work on the cross, which is the very presence of God. Last, we will explore the practical steps of how we can effectively and authentically access this power to be active participants in what God is up to today.

So, here's to the wonderfully normal ones. The ones who hold the mic *and* the ones who work forty to sixty hours a week in an office. The gifted ones with *and* without an international platform. The ones with a dream and some pocket change of hope to throw at it. The ones with a few followers on Instagram composed of family and friends. The ones who have plenty to give *and* the ones who have just enough to get by. Here's to the volunteer on the church's welcoming team. The parent who yearns to see faith bud in their children. The youth leader who spends her Friday nights throwing pizza parties and holding scavenger hunts with middle schoolers. The caregiver at home.

Here's to you.

God can do amazing things with ordinary people. Dare I say, even unlikely people. For a year, the power of the Holy Spirit surged through my sick body and looked like persistent hope and silent obedience. I was continually writing and rewriting. Continuing to serve at church. Going where He told me to go, saying what He told me to say. However, after a year of this, I experienced the power of the Holy Spirit in another way. A group of friends gathered around me during a prayer meeting and gently laid their hands on my shoulder and back. One of them said her prayer out loud for me to hear.

"I pray for healing over your body in Jesus's name."

I haven't been wallowing in bed since.

EVERYDAY, ORDINARY, AND UNLIKELY

It may feel ironic to delve into the discussion of God's power by first talking about ourselves. I can assure you that this is not a digression and will be worth the exploration. If Jesus gives you power, it's not meant to sit dormant or remain theoretical. Instead, it means He wants power to flow through you. What's often in the way isn't God but, rather, ourselves. Because the Holy Spirit will not forcefully use us without our yielded participation, we must dare to be ruthlessly honest about what's keeping us from wholeheartedly operating in the anointing of the Holy Spirit.

Before you begin the next few chapters, will you pray this prayer with me?

Heavenly Father,

No one knows me better than You do. I choose to wholly depend on Your unconditional love as I begin this journey.

Please show me what You see. Help me see how You've chosen me for the good works You planned ahead for me.

Search me and point out any lie, fear, pride, or pain that is hindering me from walking in Your power.

Teach me ways that I may live in partnership with You.

In Jesus's name I pray, amen.

1

UNASHAMEDLY WEAK

You and I are weak. It's a truth that none of us like making obvious, but hang with me here. Many of us don't like to admit that we are a breath away from breaking, stumbling, or drifting. Strip away the busy schedules, the accolades, the filtered faces, or the reputation that you cover yourself with. Remove the scaffolding you built to look like you're "enough," and what's left is the sobering truth: You are dust and breath. Acknowledging this isn't always easy, but it is the most sacred place to begin learning about God's power in you.

Most of us aren't naturally at ease with our shortcomings. We tend to hide them, deny them, or try our best to outgrow them. If given the choice, few would keep their limitations. You probably didn't choose the struggles you're battling or invite the judgments that come your way. Surely, you didn't want to make the mistakes you've made. If you could erase your history of regrets, you would. Because the truth is, none of us like sitting in the raw, vulnerable space of being flawed.

Before we go any further, it's important to pause and make a distinction between weakness and sin—because they are not the same. Sin is defiance of God's will and way, essentially an action, thought, or attitude that opposes His nature. As 1 John 3:4 reminds us, "Everyone who commits sin practices lawlessness; and sin is lawlessness." It is both a choice and condition of falling short of God's standards, and it's healed with genuine repentance. Sin is a moral failure, whereas weakness is a vulnerability that makes moral failure possible. Weakness is the condition of human limitation.

Now, why does this matter? Because some may treat sin as though it were just weakness, thereby avoiding responsibility for choices that require a confession and change of mindset and behavior. On the other hand, some may treat weakness as though it were sin, consequently trapping themselves under shame and self-condemnation. Knowing the difference sets you free because it opens the door to both accountability *and* grace.

Although your weaknesses may make you vulnerable to sin, weakness in and of itself is not a vice. For example, your weakness could be that you are prone to be tempted with inappropriate thoughts about the opposite gender. However, being prone to something and continuously entertaining a lustful imagination are different. In another example, your weakness could be your lack of leadership experience, which can lead to poor strategies and unwise choices. Sin enters when leadership is used to harm, manipulate, or gain for yourself. *Sin is something to repent of, but weakness is something to embrace to intimately know God's power.*

ACKNOWLEDGING YOUR THORNS

In 2 Corinthians 12:7–8, the apostle Paul wrote, "In order to keep me from becoming conceited, I was given a thorn in my flesh, a messenger of Satan, to torment me. Three times I pleaded with the Lord to take it away from me" (NIV). What was the thorn in Paul's flesh? Many theologians and scholars have offered educated guesses, but ultimately, no one knows with absolute certainty what the thorn was. What we can confidently presume, however, is that it distressed Paul to the point of driving him to pleading. Again, again, and again.

> Take it away from me, Lord.
> Please take it away from me.
> Take it away from me, Jesus!

What are your thorns, Friend? Have you ever found yourself begging God to take your pain away? Maybe you beseeched Him to remove an insecurity that burdened you. Perhaps it's a financial matter that's mercilessly looming over you. Maybe you have a demanding career that makes you feel ill-equipped to serve your church because you cannot attend all the events and programs that other congregants never miss. If there were a magical eraser that could wipe away your shameful past, you may be willing to pay the highest price for it.

As a pastor, I've seen many reasons as to why someone believes they can no longer attend church, participate in a believing community, or serve God. The following is not an exhaustive list, but it's some of the more common reasons I've heard:

- a messy divorce
- a bad reputation
- mental health struggles
- tragedy and loss
- a lack of spiritual hunger and passion
- a fear of failure
- doubts
- rejection from others
- physical disabilities and illness
- inadequacy
- financial difficulties

There are many blemishes we try to hide—sometimes with bravado, sometimes with rebellion. It is the part of us that we wish to dispose of because it leaves us feeling uncomfortably vulnerable. It's a brokenness that causes us to abashedly gaze at the sunny smiles of seemingly perfect Christians, wondering what it's like to have it all together. Our thorns can make us dislike ourselves. Some can even make us dislike our lives. Thorns are the great disqualifier that makes us feel as if it's our calling to simply survive because we are in no place to overflow with the power of Jesus. Instead of believing *I'm a child of God!* we may think, *I'm a failure.*

If you've ever been poked by something sharp, it's often your immediate reaction to focus on where you've been poked. That's how we are with our thorns. They make us focus on ourselves and become overwhelmed by our weaknesses. Consequently, thorns make us forget how strong and able Jesus is.

COVERING OUR WEAKNESSES

When I was a little girl, I would go to the pet store to play with the kittens. It was common for locals to drop in and let these tiny felines out of their crates to pet them. On one occasion, I saw a wide-eyed tabby scrunched into the far corner of her crate. I didn't realize that this poor kitten was likely huddled there out of fear. I reached for her without thinking, causing her to immediately hiss and swipe. The cat left a large scratch on my arm—and it left me shamefaced with embarrassment. I spent the rest of the day hiding this wound. In retrospect, I know full well that it was not that big of a deal. The cut wasn't deep, and it was a childish mistake. But somehow, in that very moment, it felt like a mark of shame. Being that I was young and, admittedly, a budding perfectionist even then, this scratch mortified me. For the next few hours, I positioned my opposite hand subtly over the scratch.

You may have scratches that you are trying to cover as well. Slow down and consider the following carefully: *What are you covering, and what are you using to cover it?*

You could be covering your inability to break free from depression with the sparkle of your talents. You could be hiding your childhood wounds with achievements and accolades. You could be concealing your insecurity with your wit and humor. Perhaps you focus on your physical appearance to project the impression that you're thriving in life, when in actuality you're inwardly falling apart. Maybe you say certain things on Facebook or post a certain picture on Instagram to prove your value to others (and maybe even yourself), when what you feel is invisible. Or perhaps your busy schedule seems productive until you realize it also leaves you no room to process your loneliness.

It's possible that you are using religion to cover your weaknesses too! Those who feel as though they have an unforgivable past may compensate by being faithful attendees at church. Perhaps you disdain your inability to overcome some of your doubts, so you make sure you look the part of a devout Christian to make up for it. You sing extra loudly to cover your shame. You smile extra brightly to cover your pain.

We can keep up with this for as long as our coverings of choice don't fail us, which they will inevitably do. They inflate us and deceive us, until they don't. When we lose them, we feel defenseless, because this is when our weaknesses are exposed. I believe many of our "coverings" were exposed during 2020, which is one of the reasons it was a deeply disorienting time for many. Those who hid behind their activities could not hide anymore. Our accomplishments and plans were no longer distractions from the conditions of our hearts, even the conditions of our relationships and communities. We had to face the reality of who we were head-on, and many of us did not like what we saw.

The funny thing is, God has seen it all along. The Holy Spirit has a 360-degree view of who you are, not just who you are trying to be. Every lack and shortcoming is in clear view. Why does He not just make it easier on us all and transform us into perfect superhumans that always do, think, and feel the right things? Why is it that He does not always change our circumstances in our favor? Why can't He just fix us so that we can be better? It is because *God isn't as offended by our weaknesses as we are.*

RECONCILING WITH YOUR WEAKNESSES

Let's continue with Paul's cry. In the next few verses, he wrote, "[The Lord] said to me, 'My grace is sufficient for you, for my power is perfected in weakness.' Therefore, I will most gladly boast all the more about my weaknesses, so that Christ's power may reside in me. So I take pleasure in weaknesses, insults, hardships, persecutions, and in difficulties, for the sake of Christ. For when I am weak, then I am strong."* Talk about a vibe change! We started this passage with Paul recollecting his desperate plea to God. And now? There's gladness and pleasure! What changed?

How did Paul overcome his disdain for his weaknesses? How did he find peace under the pressure to overcome it? You might know this pressure too—the constant push to be better, stronger, skinnier, richer, more successful, or more admired. It can come from the competitive tone at your workplace. Maybe comments from your peers and family. Perhaps you feel invisible at church because your relationship with Jesus doesn't look like anyone else's. But hear me out: *God never tells us to ignore our weakness or to compensate for what we are not.* There is no power in that.

When Moses argued that he could not speak like a leader, God did not command him to wait until he could measure up to be the sort of leader that was worthy of Israel.† When Jeremiah confessed that he was too young to fulfill his role as God's prophet, God did not tell him to power up and believe in the

* 2 Corinthians 12:9–10.

† Exodus 4:10–14.

greatness within himself.* Does it make a bit more sense now why God did not take away Paul's thorn?

When God does not remove your thorns, it's because He plans to insert Himself into the equation instead. When He does not take away obstacles, it is because He intends to show up in them. Instead of compensating for your weakness, Jesus asks you to keep following Him while trusting that He will give you everything you need to be faithful and strong in His presence. Friend, His grace will make up for what you have not measured up to. God's grace for Moses was His miracle-working power and the provision of his brother Aaron. God's grace for Jeremiah was His supernatural protection from harm and the might to face opposition.

In the New Living Translation of 2 Corinthians 12:9, God's words to Paul are, "My power works best in weakness." While you may hate your insufficiency and inadequacy, God actually prefers them. The very weakness you wish to get rid of just so happens to be the starting point for His greatest works in your life. So, you know that very part of yourself that you hate? The degree you lack? The talent you do not possess? The approval you don't have? That memory in your past you desperately wish you could change? That is the very thing setting you up to experience God's power. Yes, that's right. In Christ, weakness cannot rob you. Instead, it can only qualify you.

So, can we stop rejecting ourselves? Can we stop succumbing to the shame of our past and covering parts of who we are that we deem less acceptable? How about we present our whole selves to the Holy Spirit when we pray and not just the religiously presentable parts? How about we stop discounting

* Jeremiah 1:6–8.

ourselves for God's kingdom work just because we don't look and sound like the ones we see at the pulpit? My prayer for you is that you will have absolute peace as you survey all of who you are and who you are not.

TRADING YOUR POWER FOR HIS

Many of us exert an extensive amount of energy to outrun our limitations, perhaps even subconsciously. Here are some of the confessions I've heard over the years:

- "I learned to have a loud personality to hide the depression I struggle with."
- "I gained knowledge and learned to be articulate so that no one can make me feel like I do not belong."
- "I live to accomplish my goals to feel secure in my identity."
- "I purposely don't try my best, because if I fail, at least I can say I wasn't really trying."

Whatever we use to make up for our weakness is an alternative source of power that we've learned to lean on apart from the Holy Spirit. The first step to embracing weakness is to free ourselves from the tactics, connections, and things that offer a sense of security. It is to let go of where we draw our worldly strength. This must come first. Let's look at some examples from the Bible:

> Before the Israelites took on the great wall of Jericho, they took flint to circumcise every man that was called to fight.*

* Joshua 5.

> Before Gideon fought the Midianites, God had him reduce his army of thirty-two thousand to three hundred in order to win their battle.*
>
> Before Elijah called down fire from heaven to disprove the false prophets of Baal, he commanded the people to pour water over the wood, further increasing the impossibility of success.†
>
> Before the twelve disciples were sent to cast out demons and heal the sick, Jesus told them to take nothing for the road except a staff—no bread, bag, money, or even an extra shirt.‡

Weakness is a prerequisite for God to demonstrate His great power. It's not that He's trying to lower us to prove a point. It's that He will empower only our most authentic, barest self. The sooner we let go of whatever puffs us up to feel stronger than we actually are, the sooner we will know what only God can do. Of course, letting go of *our* power for His power doesn't need to translate to extreme actions like adult circumcision or anything along those lines. For instance, if you find that you place an unhealthy amount of security in your spouse, this does not mean that you eliminate that spouse to fully trust God's power!

But let's get practical here. How do we trade our power for His?

* Judges 7.
† 1 Kings 18.
‡ Luke 9.

1. Identify the alternative source of power you use to compensate for your weakness. What do you use to mask your flaws? What do you hide behind? Confess it to Jesus.
2. Recognize who you are when that alternative source of power is not in the picture. For example, who are you without your appearance, your reputation, or your career?
3. Break up with denial. Quit the act. Accept your need of God. If it's difficult to do, try writing down who you really are and what the state of your life really is. Recognize your thorn.
4. Ask the Holy Spirit for His perspective. What does He think about you? As you bring your realest self to Him, what are His thoughts? If you find this part difficult, go to Scripture because He speaks there too. Read passages like Psalm 139 or Matthew 10:26–31.
5. Ask Jesus to give you instructions for today or for this stage of your life. Are you to continue at your current job? Are you to reconcile with someone? If you have difficulty with this, again, open the Bible and find an instruction you see in Scripture that you can obey in this season.

Release yourself from what offers you a false sense of strength by bringing it to Jesus through confession. Access God's power through obedience. The apostle Paul brought his thorn to the Holy Spirit, and through prayer, he gained heaven's perspective of his weakness. He didn't receive a way to hide or remove it, but he remained committed to God's will and way anyway. And he did so with divine strength!

BREAKING FROM SHAME

I'm currently in the stage of life where I frequently hear about loss, failure, divorce, illness, and anything in between. When I was younger, these were rarities. However, life does what life does, and in this past year alone, I've sat with a number of friends who were shell-shocked by the sudden loss of a dream. Whether the hurt was self-incurred or forced on them by circumstance, watching someone sit in the wreckage of broken hopes is never an easy sight. We can so easily become ashamed when the evidence of our falling short is on display for others to witness. No one enjoys giving the impression that they do not have it all together.

Oftentimes in Christian culture, we tend to focus on what should be and will be instead of what is. We are quick to pull from Bible verses that remind us to "consider it pure joy"* or "be courageous!"† We eagerly push hope onto the wailing mother or the heartbroken friend. Yes, it's true, this is but a "momentary light affliction."‡ Yes, all things will work together for our good.§ But you know what's also true? Our weakness. Our brokenness. Our limitations. In the end, both glory and fallibility are undeniable realities that live within us. We must acknowledge them both, or we can allow our weakness to cloak us with shame.

Paul unashamedly proclaimed to the Corinthians that he and his fellow ministers were just clay jars that got to carry the treasure of the gospel.¶ Clay jars were likely everyday, dispos-

* James 1:2–4, NIV.
† John 16:33.
‡ 2 Corinthians 4:17.
§ See Romans 8:28.
¶ 2 Corinthians 4:7.

able earthenware containers that were sold for an extremely cheap price, perhaps even an earthenware oil lamp. They held the least value compared to other containers because, once fractured, they had no use. At least metal and glass can be fixed or repurposed.*

So, what was Paul comparing the fiery ministers of the gospel to?

- cheap,
- fragile,
- breakable,
- disposable clay containers

That's countercultural even in this day. Society doesn't hand its flowers to those who unreservedly place their shortcomings on display. That's why we strive to cover our lives with an attractive filter that says "He's crushing it" or "She's got it all figured out." But not Paul. He wasn't calling himself a boss. He wasn't telling us how he's crushing goals and conquering dreams. Instead, he was very honest about what they were enduring.

> We are afflicted in every way but not crushed; we are perplexed but not in despair; we are persecuted but not abandoned; we are struck down but not destroyed.†

In today's context, that's like shouting, "We got canceled!" "Our church got shut down!" "I got fired!" "I was abandoned by everyone!" In other words, we're just clay jars. But look at

* Colin G. Kruse, *2 Corinthians: An Introduction and Commentary,* vol. 8, Tyndale New Testament Commentaries (InterVarsity, 1987), 106.
† 2 Corinthians 4:8–9.

us—we're still here! The apostle Paul was not ashamed of his low points. He was not embarrassed by his lack. I think we could take a page out of his handbook and break free from the shame of our weakness. The shame of needing to grow from what we did not know. Of requiring rest when we grow weary. Of waging war with our mental health. Of experiencing a messy breakup. Of not having enough in our bank account. *God is not ashamed of you.* Instead, He's drawn to you! That's where true power chooses to rest.

FROM BROKENNESS TO REVIVAL: THE BARIO REVIVAL OF 1973

On October 4, 1973, a secondary school in the highlands of Bario in Sarawak, Malaysia, became heaven on earth. Solomon Bulan was a teacher at the Bario Government Secondary School, and he was meeting with the student leaders of the Christian club on a Thursday afternoon.* Although he was the spiritual adviser for this fellowship, he had been wrestling with a growing conviction of his hypocrisy and felt that he could no longer lead this group. Before twelve students, Solomon confessed to his double life of partying and drinking, assuming that it would mark the end of his spiritual leadership over them. However, much to his surprise, the opposite happened. The Holy Spirit used this man's weakness not to shame him but, rather, to show Himself in power. God revealed His presence in an undeniable way to everyone in the room. Soon, these fifteen-year-old students began confessing and repenting, and an out-

* Solomon Bulan and Lillian Bulan-Dorai, *The Bario Revival* (Kuala Lumpur, Malaysia: HomeMatters Network, 2004), 7–11.

pouring of the Holy Spirit drew a crowd of over a hundred students. This eventually became a spiritual awakening for the Kelabit people and their neighboring tribes. It marked the beginning of a profound transformation for an entire indigenous group. By the Holy Spirit's power, healing and deliverance pervaded the people, and the commonplace affinity to animism in the community was replaced with an authentic faith in the power of Jesus Christ. The impact of this revival has been remembered and celebrated for decades since.*

The Bario Revival was not sparked by an impressive sermon or an excellent strategy. It began when God's perfect power rested on a broken man's humble confession. Friend, may any hiding, pretending, and self-rejection be dismantled from your life. It's void of true power. The world may disdain your thorns, but the Holy Spirit desires to use them for fire.

PAUSE AND REFLECT

1. Which "thorn" in your life has gifted you with the opportunity for deeper dependence on the Lord?
2. What would obedience look like if you stopped waiting to become stronger and more capable first?
3. Whose approval are you trying to keep or earn by covering your weaknesses?

* Bulan and Bulan-Dorai, *The Bario Revival*, 201–16.

2

FREE TO BE UNREMARKABLE

It was testimony hour during summer youth camp, and it was my turn to share my salvation story. Public speaking came easy to me, so I wasn't nervous at all. I had my talking points well rehearsed and memorized. I stood in front of the audience of fellow students and did what I knew to do. It was a good speech, if I say so myself. I noticed some nods and smiles, so I assumed that I was doing well. After I finished sharing my testimony, I confidently walked off the stage, knowing full well that I crushed the assignment.

After my turn, another female student was next. She didn't have my confidence. She hardly knew how to hold the microphone as she found her footing by the podium. I saw her tiny frame shakily inhale as she primed herself with a big breath. But before she could even begin, she had to stop. Her face became flushed with nervousness, and after what felt like forever, she quietly but very intentionally said . . .

"I love Jesus so much."

What happened next marked me. It felt like love entered the room, and a divine weight filled the atmosphere. It was as if we all realized at the same time that this room we'd been in for an hour was actually holy ground. She continued to share, to the best of her ability, why she loved Jesus so much. It wasn't the best speech, and she continued to stumble through it. Nevertheless, after her five minutes were done, the overseeing pastor felt led to open the altar, and it became flooded with weeping middle school and high school students who were hungry for God's presence—including myself.

Although I brought to the room a well-rehearsed speech, what this young lady brought was the power of God. It was this very power that brought the proud to their knees and the broken to shout His praise. This power had nothing to do with her, and yet it also had everything to do with her. It was not the result of her effort or skill. She did not have fame or expertise to leverage her words. Ultimately, it was the anointing of the Holy Spirit, and He chose her as a conduit.

Ours is an age where power is assumed to be with the extraordinary. When we see fame, we assume influence. When we see wealth, we presume strength. We take charisma for capability, and the gifted ones can seem like God's chosen vessels. Yet the preferred resting place for God's supernatural power is not our greatness but, rather, our yieldedness.

In fact, God is not interested in our greatness. When we see how redemptive history unfolds throughout the Bible, we realize it's a story that is generally absent of the remarkable and simply filled with the willing. We can mistakenly have a sensationalized perspective of our biblical heroes. We may think that Moses was a powerful leader to emulate. David was a legendary king. Mary was chosen and set apart. While all of this is true, they were also just a condemned exile, an overlooked shepherd, and a common girl. Add to that list everyday fishermen, anonymous widows, barren women, and reviled tax collectors.

THE LIE OF SPIRITUAL EXCEPTIONALISM

The moment you believe that certain people are more chosen or favored by Jesus because of their gifts, background, knowledge, experience, or perceived spirituality, you have bought into the deceptive myth of spiritual exceptionalism. Do you ever feel like someone is more important to God's kingdom than others? Is there a church or faith group that seems to you like they are at the center of what God's doing on this earth, while the rest seem like supporting characters? Maybe it's your favorite Christian influencer that exudes #goals for you. It could be the most respected ministry in your area, the one that holds the gatherings that everyone goes to. Perhaps it's everyone's favorite worship leader at your church. Maybe it's the person with a PhD in biblical theology. It could even be the person who's always sitting in the front row on Sundays, with a notebook and tissues.

Even if these are genuinely the humblest and most Spirit-led people, it is how we compare ourselves to them that traps us in the falsehood of spiritual exceptionalism. Some may look at those who seem to be spiritual superstars and, knowingly or unknowingly, strive to become them. You may try to talk like they do. Read the same books so to be as wise as they are. Maybe you're feeling compelled to grow a social media following like they have. For others, it isn't so obvious. Maybe there's a Christian leader you are quietly idealizing because they are who you want to be. Maybe they have the life you wish you had. You may not even realize you're placing them on a pedestal and thereby identifying with them more than you identify with Christ Himself.

Now, not everyone reacts to the overcast of spiritual exceptionalism the same way. You may not be trying to be on par with "the greats," but you may be sidelining yourself from the Holy Spirit and His work instead. It can sound like this:

- "I sit in the back row because I don't feel worthy to be with these folks."
- "I see the need, but God wouldn't use someone like me."
- "God hasn't gifted me for His work because I'm not an influential person."
- "We can't do much because we are just a small ministry."
- "Can you pray for me? God hears your prayers more than mine."
- "I don't know the Bible because I'm not a pastor."

We refrain from using the spiritual gifts that God has purposefully entrusted us with because others seem to have more capability. We overlook the good work He prepared ahead of time for us, assuming someone "holier" has got it covered. We disqualify ourselves from a close friendship with Jesus because we aren't the "chosen ones." We retreat from the calling He has already equipped us for because we are not who "they" are—the supposed spiritual elite.

Church culture can feed into the lie as well. At times, without knowing it or intending it, youth ministries can overemphasize to students that they have an amazing destiny, without realizing that this one-dimensional messaging can convey that anything less than amazing is a failure of faith. Similarly, our Sunday service takeaway can be that we are called to be world changers, leaving unseasoned guests and attendees with a restless spirituality more than a love for Jesus. Now, are these ideas inherently untrue? No, not at all. Christians do have an amazing destiny and are called to be world changers. But if that's all we choose to hear, we will mistakenly pursue significance rather than faithfulness, when it's the pursuit of faithfulness that forms the most impactful believers.

The matter of spiritual exceptionalism is not new. In the days of the early church, there was a group of heretics called the Gnostics, who claimed that only the spiritual elite were privy to God's special revelation.* The apostle John aggressively refuted these people who preached that a special group had access to higher divine knowledge than others. This exceptionalism was antithetical to God's way. John made this clear by writing in 1 John 2:20, "You have an anointing from the Holy One, and all of you know the truth." Did you catch that? The special revelation of God was not reserved for an exclusive club of God's best and brightest. Instead, John said it's for "all of you." Your qualification to be an insider in God's family is the anointing of the Holy Spirit, which is the presence and power of God (we will unpack this in more depth in a later chapter). You, too, can hear from Jesus. You, too, have direct access to your heavenly Father. Yes, *you*.

It's also worth mentioning that while every believer carries the Spirit's anointing, not all anointings look the same. As is ev-

* John R. W. Stott, *The Letters of John: An Introduction and Commentary*, vol. 19, Tyndale New Testament Commentaries (InterVarsity, 1988), 110–11.

ident in the New Testament, God does choose some to take on specific roles of authority and leadership to serve the body of Christ—such as apostles, prophets, teachers, and so on. The Holy Spirit disperses gifts and responsibilities according to His wisdom, not because some are worthier than others. The reason this is not the same as spiritual exceptionalism is because being chosen to lead others doesn't automatically mean greater impact than others. These callings are assigned by God as responsibilities to serve, not as a measure of greater spiritual value and usefulness.

ORDINARY AND FAVORED

As an elementary student, I used to go to Kumon (cue the collective groan from those of you who share this memory). For those who don't know about it, Kumon is an after-school program that teaches kids math and English through repetitive worksheets. Although I didn't love extra homework, I admit, the program worked for me. I was leaps ahead of my classmates when it came to arithmetic and reading comprehension. In elementary school, being ahead in this way made me feel special, gifted even. My peers were always complimenting me, and the teachers were frequently noting my achievements. I relished being extraordinary because being set apart made me feel significant. I felt as though I had a superpower—until I reached algebra, which I immediately discovered was my kryptonite. By middle school, I tasted that humble pie and discovered that I was fairly average in academics, which helped me realize how much significance I drew from being impressive. Thankfully, what impresses people doesn't impress God at all.

In Scripture, there was something special about Saul. Take

a look at his introduction in the Bible: "There was a prominent man of Benjamin named Kish son of Abiel, son of Zeror, son of Becorath, son of Aphiah, son of a Benjaminite. He had a son named Saul, an impressive young man. There was no one more impressive among the Israelites than he. He stood a head taller than anyone else."*

Saul was a remarkable man and the son of a prominent man. Notice that the word *impressive* is used twice in these two verses. He was visually striking to the average Israelite, a head taller than anyone else. He became the very first king of Israel, and if you think about it, it made sense for him to become king. It seems that what makes a king is to be impressive, prominent, and simply more special than others. But if you know your Bible history, you know that Saul is now known as the king that failed because he rejected God's words.†

Saul, despite all his remarkability, did not have the one thing that mattered to God: a heart that yielded to God's will. Saul's greatness did not earn God's favor. Being from a respectable family did not impress the heavens. Saul's status as the most influential leader did not earn him an ounce of eternal reward. The King of kings on His highest throne was not wowed when Saul won battles. He was not moved when Saul prophesied.

Instead, God's attention was on an ordinary, overlooked shepherd boy named David. Ironically, no one else's attention was on David, not even his own father's. When Samuel the prophet showed up at Jesse's home to anoint the next king, Jesse brought out all his sons but David. Let's consider this for

* 1 Samuel 9:1–2.

† 1 Samuel 15.

a second. Samuel saw Eliab, the firstborn son, and said, "Certainly the LORD's anointed one is here before him."* Friend, Samuel was a prophet, and *still* he could not help but note how impressive Eliab was physically. Even the most faithful believers can be swayed by human distinction. This is a sobering reminder for us all.

But God?

He said, "Do not look at his appearance or his stature because I have rejected him. Humans do not see what the LORD sees, for humans see what is visible, but the LORD sees the heart."†

God looks past the pomp and circumstance. He does not consider the reputation. He is not swayed by appearances, nor is He drawn to a particular brand. The accolades. The achievements. The status. The applause. He sees through it all. It does not matter how many people like this person. It does not matter how respected someone is. The way God sees is not the way humanity sees. This means you and I must be willing to alter our vision to value what God values. Most of us have been trained to pay attention to greatness because that's where we expect to find significance. Let's begin to notice something else that looks altogether minor and ordinary to this world but precious to God, and that's faithfulness.

Take a moment and think of the most faithful friend you have. How about the most faithful member of your family? The people you are thinking of right now are not the ones who impress you with their extensive education or their plethora of connections. Instead, they are the ones who are consistently

* 1 Samuel 16:6.

† 1 Samuel 16:7.

present. They show up for both the big moments and the small moments. They respond to your texts and pick up when you call. There's an enduring loyalty that is felt, even though it may be quiet. This is what I mean when I say faithfulness looks ordinary and is easily overlooked.

Saul was a decorated king with the fanfare of followers around him. Yet, after his disobedience, God's eyes were drawn to a run-of-the-mill shepherd boy. David was a handsome young man, but he otherwise had nothing that sparkled, nothing that drew particular attention. Even his own father neglected to send for him when the prophet came. Nevertheless, he was God's favored choice.

It's a wonder how we are all trying to be what God's not *looking for.* Most of us are trying to "make it" to whatever destination has the most likes, promotions, and acknowledgments. We do the same with our Christian faith as well. We start to equate hype with a move of the Holy Spirit, big accomplishments with a sign of His blessing, and the approval of people with the favor of God Himself. So, whether we are aware of it or not, we find ourselves striving to conjure up faith to be better, gain more, and get big things done, when this is contrary to how Jesus actually lived.

One of the most humbling moments of my family's life was when we were starting a church during 2020. For at least fifteen years up until that point, my husband and I were church leaders and pastors. Although we were never trying to be, we were somebodies to some people because of our standing in the faith community. We lived a life that had a consistent rhythm of accomplishments—goals were being met and the church was growing. We had titles and a measurable purpose in life. A busy schedule felt like proof that we were doing something right. However, when we took the step of faith to start a church in 2020 and an unexpected lockdown due to a global pandemic came about, we got a reality check. Without the people around to affirm us or the growing ministry to approve us, what were we? For the rest of that year, we didn't have a church building, an income, a community, or a ministry. For the first time in many years, we were just people. We were neighbors on our street. Shoppers at the grocery store. Taxpaying citizens of our town. I did not realize just how much strength I was gleaning from being a leader who got stuff done. It was uncomfortable for quite some time—until it became liberating.

THE COURAGE TO BE ORDINARY

In today's world of highlight reels, milestone chasing, and dream building, it takes more faith to be ordinary than to become extraordinary. I've listened to youth group students who were anxious to fulfill their God-given potential. I've sat with preachers who were wrestling with the timing of when they would preach to the nations. I've witnessed the tears of regret from those who felt they missed God's timing for their calling. It's the by-product of being in that never-ending race to "get there" and "arrive," because here and right now doesn't measure up. It doesn't feel right to stay in the same old town. There must be more than this nine-to-five desk life or this part-time gig that isn't exactly what I want to be doing but still pays the bills.

There's nothing wrong with a healthy dose of ambition, nor did God design us to live our lives ignoring growth, excellence, and fruitfulness. However, let's explore where that healthy ambition is supposed to be rooted. In the Garden of Eden, Adam and Eve were created in the image of God. As His direct representatives on earth and stewards of His glory, the commission to "be fruitful, multiply, fill the earth, and subdue it"* was in the context of Adam and Eve expanding and growing God's dominion on earth. It wasn't that Adam and Eve needed to make something of their lives. They weren't told to go and be fruitful so they could chase after some greater meaning or purpose. Instead, everything was for God's dominion.

Yet somewhere after the rebellion and fall of humankind in the garden, people became distracted with the pursuit of significance, because significance gave them a false sense of power. Instead of living from an overflow of intimate friendship with our Creator, people began living to be someone or to achieve something. Even Christians today can obsess over their life calling—not to glorify God but instead to find their own place on earth. We can observe how humankind inevitably lost its way when they eventually said, "Come, let's build ourselves a city and a tower with its top in the sky. Let's make a name for ourselves."† A people who were meant to live to reflect God's glory now lived to shine like God, to become more than what they were. We read of how God dismantled their plan in the rest of Genesis 11, and then, immediately afterward in Genesis 12, He gave a great blessing to a man named Abram.

> The LORD said to Abram:
> Go from your land,
> your relatives,
> and your father's house

* Genesis 1:28.

† Genesis 11:4.

> to the land that I will show you.
> I will make you into a great nation,
> I will bless you,
> I will make your name great,
> and you will be a blessing.
> I will bless those who bless you,
> I will curse anyone who treats you with contempt,
> and all the peoples on earth
> will be blessed through you.*

What a contrast here! The scene changed from Genesis 11 to 12 just like that! We see how God treated a mass of people who were scrambling to make their mark on this earth. And then we see how God delivered a blessing of greatness to this ordinary man. One can assume that Abram truly was ordinary. There is absolutely no fantastic descriptor given for him. No memorable physical characteristics. No regimen that he lived by. No achievement. Nothing impressive about his personality. The only things that are mentioned in his introduction to God's narrative in Genesis are that he was the son of Terah, the uncle to Lot, and the husband to Sarai, who was barren. He was a common man, living a common life. He likely spent each day overseeing his livestock, managing household business, problem-solving the issues of the community, learning to live with the reality that he may never have his own biological son, and so on.

But he did do this *one* thing. Genesis 12:4 says,

> Abram went, as the LORD had told him.

* Genesis 12:1–3.

Abram, later known as Abraham, listened to God's voice and obeyed—aka good old everyday faithfulness. Let's not miss the beauty in this detail. Abraham had grown up in a polytheistic environment.* His father worshipped other gods. Abraham did not even come from a home that revered Yahweh! Yet when Abraham heard God, he responded to what God said. Abraham stopped for Him. He made space for His voice. He took His directions seriously. He even changed his whole life to take God at His word. An ordinary man chose to believe that Yahweh was extraordinary, and that changed everything! We still remember his name to this day, and the Lord allowed his legacy to live on for generations. Meanwhile, we don't know a single name of those who were trying to build the Tower of Babel.

So, let's think about this, Friend. Are you living the Tower of Babel sort of life—consumed by the need to build significance while leaving no impact on redemptive history? Or are you living as Abraham did—faithful to one's everyday duties and roles while honoring God? N. T. Wright wrote, "The church's job is not to create its own version of the success stories the world tells. It's to point to the true story, the one in which God's power is made perfect in weakness, and where the final victory belongs to those who love and serve, not those who win and dominate."†

Once, while attending a prayer meeting, I was kneeling before the Lord and having my personal time with Him. Suddenly, someone I hardly knew at the time came over to me and prayed

* Joshua 24:2.

† N. T. Wright, *After You Believe: Why Christian Character Matters* (HarperCollins, 2010), 35.

these words aloud: "You stand in a line of legacy. Your great-grandfather was able to see the movements to come." I was floored by what she said. I had met her briefly before the prayer meeting began, and just then, she told me something that could have come only from the Holy Spirit. My great-grandfather was a church planter in South Korea back when it wasn't really called being a "church planter." He started churches in the heart of Buddhist towns, and his routine was to take my mother, his granddaughter, with him to sweep the floors to prepare for early morning prayer. My mother, even when she was not a believer, fondly recalled these sweet memories of following her grandfather to the church and watching him do what he always did: serve and pray. I always found this part of our family history fascinating because who knew that generations later, his great-granddaughter would also plant a church on a different land. For years, I wondered if he had known what the impact of his faith would be. God, in His divine kindness, gave me a gift that day through this praying woman. I stand on the shoulders of an ordinary man. He dedicated his quiet life to daily obedience, and the Holy Spirit took it from there.

Sometimes, it's not tragedy that discourages our faith. It's mundanity. We get pumped to believe in an almighty Jesus on Sunday and still have to do our laundry and taxes on Monday. We can mistake repetitive routines as a lack of progress. An uneventful day can feel like an absence of faith. Can we release ourselves from the pressure to prove, perform, and produce something noteworthy? Can we wash the dishes and go to work without resenting the monotony of it all? The quiet moments are not in the way of your dreams. You are allowed to quit the race for greater significance. Today, I challenge you to celebrate the most ordinary, unremarkable, and common aspects about you and your life. After all, they are what Jesus came to redeem and where the Spirit has made His dwelling.

PAUSE AND REFLECT

1. What emotions rise in you when others receive the opportunities or acknowledgment that you hope for? What do these emotions reveal?
2. Where in your life are you resisting God's invitation into everyday, ordinary faithfulness?
3. What are some expectations you have for yourself that you may have mistaken as God's expectations for you?

3

UNSEEN, UNWANTED, AND AT PEACE

It was my third time running for class president. I was in seventh grade. The first two times were in different schools, and I always landed the vice president spot—second best. I rather enjoyed it, though. I didn't mind speaking in public, solving problems, "leading the way," so to speak. So, it felt very natural to run again when I was in a new school with new kids. I delivered a well-thought-out speech and gave it my best shot. On election day, the much-anticipated announcement came over the intercom, and again, I was the runner-up.

Being that I was relatively naïve and optimistic at the age of thirteen, I didn't give it a second thought. However, a classmate came up to me during free hour and said, "You should have won. You deserved it. It's just how things are, you know? She's just way more popular than you." This was the first time I was made aware of my lack of popularity. His well-intentioned but slightly offhanded remark woke me up to something I was unaware of until then. Later, I learned from classmates that while I was working on my speech and putting up posters, my opponent was garnering favor with our classmates—going from table to table during lunchtime and convincing everyone to vote for her. To her credit, she understood politics better than I. However, at that time I felt the sting of being unwanted and the consequences of being unseen.

From then on, I made an internal pact that I would always be the funniest, most well-spoken, and best-dressed person in any room. I never wanted to be robbed of what was rightfully mine just because someone did not see me or know me. I created a likable persona. I learned how to be useful and valuable to people so that they would not reject me. It was my way of protecting myself and ensuring my way forward. As a Christian, I transferred this false thinking into my faith journey and believed that I needed to be seen, heard, and accepted by others to make a difference in the world. I lived with this belief until it burned me out. It turns out, there's no power in living that way.

THE NEED TO BE SEEN

Public approval is not a qualification in the kingdom of God. In fact, there is no spiritual value tied to recognition and renown. From heaven's perspective, it is not a standard for greatness. While our culture prizes the viral ones, the up-and-comers, and the most sought-after, the Holy Spirit works mightily through obscurity. Consider the following examples:

Shiphrah and Puah, the Hebrew midwives, quietly defied the order of Pharaoh and ensured the safe delivery of Israelite boys, securing the continuation of God's people.*

The nameless widow of Zarephath cared for the prophet Elijah with the last bit of her flour and oil, thereby witnessing God's provision and resurrection power.†

A Roman officer amazed Jesus with his faith.‡

A boy offered his five loaves and two fish, making the great miracle of feeding the thousands possible.§

Simon of Cyrene, a random passerby, had the eternal honor of carrying Jesus's cross and sharing the burden of his savior in His final hours.¶

Hebrews 11:35–38 refers to unnamed saints, saying, "The world was not worthy of them."**

These are just a few people in the Bible who played pivotal roles in God's miracles and breakthroughs but barely had their names mentioned. Some are given a few verses at most. They are not the biblical heroes we name our children after. And

* Exodus 1.
† 1 Kings 17.
‡ Luke 7:1–10.
§ John 6:9.
¶ Mark 15:21.
** Hebrews 11:38.

quite frankly, even the biblical heroes that we *do* acknowledge today were stripped of their accolades and renown before they were usable to God. Before becoming the great leader of Israel, Moses had to leave the palace to become an anonymous shepherd. Before he sat on his seat of power, Joseph had to be stripped of his robe of favor and become both slave and prisoner. God seems to prefer the hidden ones, the unwanted ones. He handpicks His heroes in the margins.

Does your internal dialogue ever sound anything like this?

- *I can't do it because I'm no [insert the name of the most respected Christian you know].*
- *If God gave me these gifts, shouldn't I use them on a bigger platform?*
- *I want to do something that matters, not just serve in the background.*
- *I'm meant for more than this.*
- *I'm just waiting for doors to open before I really do what I'm called to do.*

We think this way when we believe the fallacy that acknowledgment and elevation are the pathways to making a noteworthy impact for Jesus. It's not about being popular or famous. For many, the need to be seen isn't just about being visible to many people; it's deeper than garnering people's attention. It's about being known and valued for who you are, whether it be from a crowd or from the two or three that you truly respect. It's the pat on the back for trying your best. The feeling when people finally recognize your gifts. When friends make space for you and include you in their activities. When you share your most vulnerable stories and are met with authentic empathy and kindness instead of judgment.

The desire to be authentically seen and known isn't wrong. It was placed in us by God because we were designed to be communal beings. However, this need is meant to be satisfied by His holy affection instead of humankind's fleeting attention. Nevertheless, we tend to misplace this longing by clamoring to be recognized, understood, and acknowledged by people instead. This endless chase can leave us feeling unwanted and unworthy, even enough to disqualify ourselves from being vessels of God's great work on earth.

We may not realize it, but the ache to be seen can quietly drive our daily behavior. The way we conduct ourselves in social spaces is telling. You may be a yes-man at your workplace because, for you, to be needed is to affirm your standing there. You may be really attached to a social cause or movement not just because you care about the matter but also because it allows you to belong to something or some people. Maybe you exaggerate your stories so that you can garner attention for a little while longer.

Let's be real—this also plays out in the church. Your eagerness to join the welcoming team may start as an avid desire to serve Jesus and His people, but it may eventually be carried by the hopes for people to acknowledge you. You may have a God-given voice to sing, but you may become frustrated that no one else acknowledges its worth or invites you to lead the congregation in worship. Does that mean God has not chosen you either? What if you have the gift to lead but no one to lead? What if you have wisdom to share but no one is listening? With the way church culture is today, it's easy to assume that the seen and recognized are the ones who are favored by God to do the good work, while those in the shadows are the ones destined for a supporting role.

Jesus was effective on this earth not because He captivated the attention of people. Isaiah 53:2 says, "He didn't have an impressive form or majesty that we should look at him, no appearance that we should desire him." You mean that Jesus did not walk around with a chiseled jawline and main-character energy? Y'all—Jesus is God! He did not lack majesty and brilliance, and He could have displayed that radiant splendor while He was ministering on earth. Yet He chose to be absolutely, unapologetically forgettable. Notice that Isaiah's prophecy never says that Jesus was flawed. This means that God rejected the chance to have all the traits that would make Him attractive and wanted by humankind, and He *still* did not lack a thing.

Popularity is not a virtue. Being sought after does not add to your value. People's acclaim cannot make you more like Christ. According to Isaiah's prophecy, Jesus chose to be unimpressive. If we were there during Jesus's ministry on earth, I wonder, would we have recognized how special He was? Would we have seen Him for what He is worth?

EMBRACING OUR ROLE

Though the world may reject you, don't reject yourself if you want to be an effective player on God's team. As a minister, I've learned this lesson the hard way. For the first decade of ministry, I found myself juggling the vast array of people's expectations of me. Some wanted an inspirational visionary leader. Others wanted the gifted preacher who delivers every Sunday. Then there were those who wanted the therapist, the pastoral friend who answers all texts, or the empathetic spiritual mother with a patient, nurturing presence. Maybe there's a minister out there who can be all these things. I, however, could not, and the rejection that came from not being able to do it all stung. After a while, the pressure to be everything for everyone got to me. It sapped me of all strength because I was preoccupied with becoming what everyone wanted. I was no longer serving God and instead became focused on pleasing people and appeasing their emotions.

Let me make this one thing very clear: The Holy Spirit has no interest in empowering you to meet everyone's expectations. This is probably why I felt so empty of power for so long. I had to take a few months to become ruthlessly honest with myself about how I'm meant to serve Jesus.

The Holy Spirit intends to use *you*, not some imitation that you're scrambling to become. Not the version of you you're trying to be so that the church values you. When we believe that other people are better fit to serve Jesus than we are, we bypass the opportunity to walk as powerful children of God. Christians tend to conjure up an idealized vision of who the worthiest candidates are to inherit God's wisdom and power. You may think that it's the most vocal one in your small group. Maybe you think it's the one who can pray out loud in front of everyone with no problem. Deep down, you may think that the one who seems to have life all figured out is God's vessel of choice. But Jesus also chose you.

This sort of elitism has been a problem since the church began. First Corinthians 12:20–24 says,

> As it is, there are many parts, but one body. The eye cannot say to the hand, "I don't need you!" Or again, the head can't

> say to the feet, "I don't need you!" On the contrary, those parts of the body that are weaker are indispensable. And those parts of the body that we consider less honorable, we clothe these with greater honor, and our unrespectable parts are treated with greater respect, which our respectable parts do not need. Instead, God has put the body together, giving greater honor to the less honorable.

The apostle Paul dealt with this issue head-on. He saw in the church what we still see today: that people believe there are some roles and positions in the body of Christ that inherently have more value than others, to the point where people will disdain their own roles and covet others. But the Holy Spirit has infinite ways by which He can use us. He can evangelize through the kind service of a crossing guard in the morning before school. He can prophesy through the encouragement of an Uber driver. He can heal through the prayers of someone sitting in the back row of church. Yet we limit Him with our belief of whom He will use.

How much more effective would we be in bringing the lost home if we would learn how to honor each body part as the Lord willed for us from the start? What if the ones with the gift of hospitality can envision house parties that host the presence of God? What if the creatives see the kingdom value in their graphic designs and music? What if the tech guy is unshakably aware of the anointing of the Holy Spirit as he is troubleshooting a network outage? Is God so unimaginative that the Holy Spirit moves only when there's a gifted orator with a microphone and a worship team to accompany?

Let me tell you about a guy named Gene. My husband and I like to say that he's one of the most important people in our church. His role? He sets up our church signs every Sunday. He serves and encourages every week. A month before we launched our church, half our team came down with Covid-19. It felt impossible to move forward. So, Dave and I prayed a very specific prayer: *Lord, please bring us more people who love the church and want to build one.* The next week, we met Gene. Team morale was down. That week, we stood in the dark rented-out AMC theater, wondering if we could really pull this off. Did we have enough lights? Would people even find this room since it was tucked away in the back of the theater? But Gene, this guy we had just met, looked around with a beaming smile and proclaimed, "This is going to be great!" That one word of encouragement pierced through the hopelessness. It was the umph we needed to take the next step, and he's been encouraging us ever since. Every week, he'd be at church before anyone else, and as he gathered signs to set up outside, he'd say simple things like "God is so good!" or "We're so blessed here. I can feel it!" On occasion, my husband and I would get a text from him saying, "I'm so thankful for you. I'm praying for you!" Let me tell you, those encouragements were an instrument of the Holy Spirit, and they were used by God to keep us going. They loved us back to life through some very dark weeks.

Gene didn't have to be like anyone else in the body of Christ. He was a servant who regularly prayed, and that's it. He did not have to manufacture greater kingdom impact by trying to lead like someone else. He did not have to wait for God to open doors, fulfill his potential, and break through to new levels to do what he did.

It's important to note that Gene is very comfortable with who he is as well. He does not feel the need to be anyone but himself. He simply gave Jesus his yes, and the Holy Spirit used it to build a church. We will never fulfill our role in God's army if we are devaluing ourselves or looking down on our stories. This is why you must embrace your God-given design and have peace with where God has placed you. Does this make you selfish if you try to do more or be more? Not at all. Accepting your unique set of skills and gifts frees you to grow without grasping. Recognizing your current assignment as God-given doesn't mean your dreams can't expand. On the contrary, it frees you from pressure to move forward with purpose. Accepting your current realm of influence doesn't mean you're not called to more. Instead, it means you trust Him to lead you there in His way, without self-consuming striving.

Friend of God, the Holy Spirit in you is alive, active, and full of good intention. He's not dwelling with you because He's got nothing else to do! He's not on retainer to be your spiritual 911 for desperate situations. The Creator of the universe and the Savior of the world chose you as His vessel, His abode on earth. You may not have made it onto the basketball team or church praise band. You may not have been asked to be the keynote speaker for any conference. However, you are handpicked by Jesus to be a representative of His will and way right *now*—right where you are. To believe you don't have a worthwhile part in His story is simply to choose to disagree with God Himself.

YOU ARE FREE—TO BE MISUNDERSTOOD

When you're at peace with being unseen and unwanted, you gain voracious courage to live in obedience to God. You pray less about people understanding you and more about people seeing Jesus. No longer are months and years spent trying to make sense of the church rejection, community gossip, or peer disapproval you've experienced. You don't build your schedule around keeping people happy. You stand for what's pure and true, even when it's more socially acceptable to compromise. You show kindness to your co-workers even though you're goaded to be vengeful. You worship with utter abandon, no matter the onlookers. Let them look. Let them judge. Let them play the guessing game of what's supposedly wrong with you. You live for Jesus, no matter what it looks like. In his book *Practicing the Power,* Sam Storms says, "Obedience must matter more to you than success or your image."*

Why am I going on about obedience? Because that's how we access the power of the Holy Spirit. Let's look at a few examples from Scripture:

> Bezalel and Oholiab did not have the wisdom and creative ability to design the tent of meeting, the ark of the covenant, or any of the holy items for worship on their own. It came to them by the Holy Spirit when they obeyed the calling to be His skilled artisans.†

> Gideon was not brave enough, or even convicted enough, to be a military leader that defeated the Midianites. It was the Spirit that enveloped him as he went by the command of God.‡

* Sam Storms, *Practicing the Power: Welcoming the Gifts of the Holy Spirit in Your Life* (Zondervan, 2017), 25.

† Exodus 31:1–6.

‡ Judges 6:34.

> Mary did absolutely nothing to make the conception of Jesus happen. She simply said yes, and the Holy Spirit created the miracle.*

The ability to win in spiritual warfare, feed thousands, walk on water, and heal the sick does not come from one's extensive knowledge of theology. It does not come from years of experience at church. It is not the fruit of piety, nor is it evidence of people's approval. The Holy Spirit flexes His strength through those who come alongside Jesus with a willingness to listen to His words and act on His instructions with faith. In other words, supernatural power is released from our obedience to Jesus.

What is keeping you from this kind of obedience? It took some time for me to realize that most of my hesitations about starting a church community in 2020 were based on the fear of what our obedience would look like to others. I remember walking the dog one afternoon ruminating about all the what-ifs. It was a humid day, and I was already irritated by the bees and mosquitoes flying about. Yet all I could think about was, *What if I fail? What if people do not want to join us? Will we be okay with starting with nothing? Will we be okay with living more frugally—not getting that new car or that fancy vacation?* I diverted from my usual walking path and went on and on (much to my Shih Tzu's delight). Somewhere along my wandering, I felt a quiet interruption of my thoughts.

My child, will you help build My church?

The bees kept buzzing and the mosquitoes kept circling and the humidity was still stifling. But my heart fell quiet. His words landed ever so delicately in my heart, but they lingered with

* Luke 1:26–38.

weighty peace. My Father is also my King. It sounded like a request, but I would have been foolish to consider it anything less than a command.

Spoiler alert—I said yes. I said yes to building a church and enduring years of rejection that followed. I said yes to a humbling budget, to insufficient help, and to subpar meeting spaces. But in that yes, lives were saved, bodies healed, and hearts delivered out of darkness. In that yes were supernatural miracles of provision and stories that not only encouraged us but set thousands free as I shared them on other pulpits. This yes gave me a kingdom adventure of a lifetime, and we're just getting started because we made peace with being unwanted and unseen.

How about you? Are you free to fully obey God, regardless of how it looks? It's not easy to accept rejection, and unnoticed faithfulness can seem like wasted effort. Yet this is the cost of wholeheartedly following Jesus. What would obedience look like for you today? Consider the ways you may be compromising for the sake of being wanted and seen by others. Turn them into a welcome confession before Jesus.

PAUSE AND REFLECT

1. Are there lies from past rejections that you still hold on to and believe to this day? How has that influenced the way you live for Jesus?
2. What emotions arise when you feel misunderstood by people? How do those emotions affect your faith?
3. If you are fully free from the need to be seen, heard, or acknowledged, what would success look like for you?

ANOINTED

As a follower of Christ, you have God's power. Even so, does God's power flow through you? Does it mark everything you do? Technically, God can handle His mission on His own. He doesn't lack angelic reinforcements or heavenly wisdom. Still, He entrusts us with His presence and power—not to use us like a puppeteer but to provide for us as His friends. Jesus says in John 15:15–16,

> I do not call you servants anymore, because a servant doesn't know what his master is doing. I have called you friends, because I have made known to you everything I have heard from my Father. You did not choose me, but I chose you. I appointed you to go and produce fruit and that your fruit should remain, so that whatever you ask the Father in my name, he will give you.

Only a gracious and kind King would choose to work with friends instead of slaves. This isn't about getting you to fulfill a checklist of deeds He wants you to accomplish. On the contrary, our Father wants to share His heart with you. He wants to show you what He sees. He wants your participation. The Holy Spirit doesn't dwell within you to control you like a chess piece. Instead, He wants to equip you to partner with Him.

God's power is different from what humans typically try to wield. It does not manipulate and take. It serves and gives. It does not operate in domination and control. Instead, it moves in love, humility, and truth. God's power is what accomplishes His work and will on this earth. It's a gift placed in every believer, and we call it anointing.

The anointing of the Holy Spirit is often thought of as mysterious, out of reach, and reserved for a few special people. In truth, it is the living presence and power of the Holy Spirit. It's an empowerment that every follower of Christ carries but that can also be ignored. My goal in the following chapters is to provide a clear foundation for understanding this power, thereby paving the way for the anointing to be your personal reality for the good of others and the glory of God.

4

POWER IS A PERSON

"When he walks in the room, the atmosphere shifts." When I heard someone describe a certain evangelist this way, my young, unseasoned ears, still adjusting to churchspeak, perked up. "What do you mean exactly?" I asked.

"Well," my friend continued, "suddenly, you feel like there's electricity in the air. People start to accept Jesus as their Lord and Savior. Some others start to weep. People start to get healed."

I had just begun to consider myself a Christian, and this sounded bizarre and otherworldly to me. But over time, I heard enough anecdotes and stories to grasp that there were some Christians who lived more powerfully than others.

Around that time, I became a part of a friend group that was on fire for Jesus. Typically, my idea of fun on a Saturday night was to go to the movies or hang out at the mall. However, this group wanted to go to parks and public spaces to look for those with crutches, casts, eye patches, or wheelchairs because they wanted to pray for healing. As the newbie of the group, I did a lot of watching, and I immediately felt powerless. How did they know to pray for that one person? How did they know what to pray for? Where did they get the boldness to do this? It led to even more questions:

- How does a foster mom protect her home and heart from darkness with her daily prayers?
- How does an addict get set free and use his story to set others free as well?
- How does someone come out of the prayer closet with a God-given plan?
- How does a teen who feels prompted to share the gospel in the school cafeteria wind up bringing the room to Jesus?
- How does an accountant know how to encourage a co-worker during break?

As a new believer, I was impressed by those who were able to move a room and inspire people. I was amazed by those who seemed to have a library of supernatural testimonies. The ones who were well read and able to articulate deep biblical revelations seemed to be in a different league, and I thought I had to know more and be better to join them. But over time, I've grown to understand that it's not the person doing it that is responsible for these abilities. God's power isn't some entity to acquire with sharp discipline or well-read knowledge. Instead, power has always been a Person.

KNOWING THE HOLY SPIRIT

From the very beginning, before time itself, He was there. He hovered over chaos and breathed life into dust, calling them His children. But dust dared to rebel, and yet He's pursued us ever since. With fire and cloud, He led Israel. With supernatural wisdom and insight, He empowered prophets, judges, and kings. He endowed craftsmen with divine skill and messengers with truth. He filled the temple with holy glory so weighty, it dropped priests to the ground. Though humanity failed again and again, nothing could stop the force of His unrelenting love. Even when we made it utterly hopeless to know Him, He made a way. He never stopped unveiling the heart of the Creator.

And when the time was right, His power overshadowed the womb of a woman named Mary. He descended like a dove at Jesus's baptism, led Him into the wilderness, filled His ministry with power for the miraculous, and raised Him from the grave. At Pentecost, He came to dwell not just among us but within us. As He once moved through Jesus, He now moves through us. He stirs compassion in once-calloused hearts. He creates miracles through our undeserving hands. He spreads the good news through lips that once cursed and lied. And all of it is possible not because we are worthy but because Jesus made us clean. Rebels made of dust have become holy temples of the One who's been around from the beginning, before time itself—the Holy Spirit.

Have you met Him? Do you know Him?

Let's take a moment to acknowledge our pure, kind, and long-suffering Friend. After all, He's with you right now. Go ahead. Close your eyes (if it's safe to) and breathe deep. Give Him an offering of your attention. Remember who He is. Helper,

Creator, Teacher, Intercessor, to name a few. He moves like wind and ignites like fire. He is living water, and He gives life to whoever embraces Him. He convicts the world of its sin. He arms His children with spiritual gifts. He *is* Power, and He adores you so. Say a greeting to Him if you wish. Sit in this moment of appreciating who He is and move on when you are ready.

The Holy Spirit and His power are not two separate entities. In other words, power cannot be separated from God. He is the strength to overcome temptation. He is the wisdom to share the gospel with a skeptical friend. He is the breaker of curses. He maneuvers circumstances that we cannot move on our own. He transforms unchangeable people. He heals both physical bodies and souls. He turns mundane moments into love encounters with His presence. He gives visions. He speaks to us in dreams. Through Him, the church set-up team that clears tables and moves chairs can prophesy. Through Him, you can shake nations through your prayers on a bus ride, in a classroom, or in hospice.

For the everyday Christian to walk in spiritual power, it's important to understand the personhood of the Holy Spirit, or else we end up treating Him like energy to accrue instead of a King to submit to. He's not some resource to fuel our hopes and dreams. Neither is He our good-luck charm for the day. The Holy Spirit is not a vending machine that gives us our healing and breakthrough when we put in enough of our songs and spiritual disciplines. We dishonor Him when we forget that He can be grieved, resisted, and lied to. He has a will and thoughts of His own. We do not pull power from heaven to wield on earth. Instead, we yield to Power—the Holy Spirit—and allow Him to wield us on earth.

THE HOLY SPIRIT'S PRESENCE AND POWER: THE ANOINTING

One of my earliest missional assignments from God was when I was a senior in high school and I was asked by my parents' friends to lead a small group Bible study for their children. We met every Saturday evening and called it Saturday Night Bible Study. I was still relatively young in my faith, so I'm not sure how this role was entrusted to me. I'd never led any spiritual gathering before, but I was the one in charge of keeping the kids occupied with activities in the basement while the adults had their own Bible study in the living room. I did not see myself as a leader by any means, but I also felt the responsibility to care for my younger friends. So I began making phone calls to them throughout the week. I made a list of all their names, and I started to check in on them, encourage them, and pray for them regularly. When making these calls, I experienced something I'd never felt before. As they would share about their doubts and struggles, I knew exactly how to respond. Specific Bible verses would come to mind, and I would share them. These regular calls helped strengthen their souls and fortify their faith—and mine too. I would somehow know what they needed to hear, to the point where sometimes they'd respond, "Whoa, it's like you're reading my mind." I knew I wasn't reading their minds. Instead, seventeen-year-old Faith was being empowered by the Holy Spirit to prophetically encourage her friends.

The Holy Spirit is the presence of God. He is not a representative of God but, rather, God Himself who dwells with and within followers of Jesus. If Jesus is seated at the right hand of

God,* then how can He also dwell in our hearts?† It is through the indwelling of the Holy Spirit. Once you choose to be a Christian, the Holy Spirit makes your very being both His temple to reside in and His vessel to move through. The presence of the Holy Spirit is also power, and this is what we call the anointing. He *is* the anointing and *gives* the anointing to every believer.

The anointing is God's presence and power for believers of Jesus Christ to set them apart and equip them for God's work.

It is what made a group of 120 people praying in an upper room, most of their names unknown, burst into different languages so that they were able to take the gospel to the ends of the earth.‡ It's how Paul's handkerchief and Peter's shadow were able to cast out demons and heal the sick.§ It is how all believers can grow in divine knowledge of a holy God.¶ It is a supernatural power endowed on followers of Jesus—not because of anything they've done to earn it but simply because Christ's blood made them worthy to carry it. How did a hodgepodge group of men and women that consistently shared meals and prayed together usher in an unstoppable holy revolution that is still spreading like wildfire across the globe today? It is the anointing of the Holy Spirit.

The anointing manifests through us in various ways. Although He is God, Jesus came to us as a man, demonstrating to us how a human can host the Holy Spirit. After all, He was called the Messiah, which means "anointed one." Isaiah 11:1–2

* Hebrews 1:3.
† Galatians 2:20.
‡ Acts 1:8; 2:4.
§ Acts 5:15–16; 19:11–12.
¶ 1 John 2:20.

offers a glimpse into how the anointing of the Holy Spirit was visible in Jesus's life while He was on earth and, by extension, how it can be made visible through Christians today. It says,

> Then a shoot will grow from the stump of Jesse,
> and a branch from his roots will bear fruit.
> The Spirit of the LORD will rest on him—
> a Spirit of wisdom and understanding,
> a Spirit of counsel and strength,
> a Spirit of knowledge and of the fear of the LORD.

This does not mean that there were seven different spirits; rather it refers to sevenfold aspects of the one Holy Spirit. However, the Spirit of the Lord, of wisdom, understanding, counsel, strength, knowledge, and fear of the Lord are not merely traits but ways the anointing actively operated in Jesus's life—and thereby in ours as well. Are these the only ways God's power manifests through us? Not at all! As a rule of thumb, I avoid putting God in a formula or system so He'll make sense to me. We can use passages like Isaiah 11:1–2 to give us a snapshot of how the anointing works in different, practical ways. It's not to say that the Holy Spirit is limited to these expressions alone. Simply put, the same anointing on Jesus now lives in us through the Holy Spirit, enabling us to walk in divine insight, ability, and reverent obedience just like He did.

1. The Spirit of the Lord

The Spirit of the Lord is the divine personhood of the Holy Spirit who reveals His presence and exercises His authority. When someone chooses to be God's child by grace through faith, the Spirit of the Lord regenerates their dead soul, giving them new life. Then we become spiritually living children of God with delegated authority. Someone who was once destined for destruction now has the Spirit of the Lord, giving them permission and power to preach the gospel. We can look on the face of sickness and have the courage to pray for healing. By His power, we have authority against evil spirits and are equipped for spiritual warfare.

In Luke 4:18–19, Jesus referred to Himself when He read in the temple:

> The Spirit of the Lord is on me,
> because he has anointed me
> to preach good news to the poor.
> He has sent me
> to proclaim release to the captives
> and recovery of sight to the blind,
> to set free the oppressed,
> to proclaim the year of the Lord's favor.

2. The Spirit of Wisdom

The Spirit of Wisdom empowers believers with divine insight and the ability to apply God's truth with creative skill. When God anointed the artisans with the Spirit of Wisdom, He said to Moses in Exodus 28:3, "You are to instruct all the skilled artisans, whom I have filled with a spirit of wisdom, to make Aaron's garments." It's not just about having more insight but also about knowing how to apply it. It is what empowers a prayerful entrepreneur to build a business that generously applies kingdom principles and excellence. The Spirit of Wisdom enables a believer to know Scripture and how to apply it to everyday life.

3. The Spirit of Understanding

The Spirit of Understanding gives supernatural discernment to a believer, which is the ability to see matters with God's perspective. This is the reason why some people can look at absolute chaos with hope and know exactly what God is up to. It's also why some people can look at someone's dark disposition and know whether it's demonic or not. Daniel was able to interpret visions and dreams of every kind because God gave him understanding.* Job 32:8 says, "It is the spirit in a person—the breath from the Almighty—that gives anyone understanding."

4. The Spirit of Counsel

The Spirit of Counsel imparts God's strategy and direction into a believer. It's what gave Joseph the ability to offer strategic counsel to Pharaoh, to the point where Pharaoh proclaimed, "Can we find anyone like this, a man who has God's spirit in him?"† It's the power that comes on someone who takes a moment to internally cry out to God in the middle of a parenting challenge and starts to sense the practical next steps to get through it. John 14:26 says, "The Counselor, the Holy Spirit, whom the Father will send in my name, will teach you all things and remind you of everything I have told you."

5. The Spirit of Strength

The Spirit of Strength is God's great impartation of ability and might for the believer to fulfill God's purpose on earth. Under

* Daniel 1:17.

† Genesis 41:38.

this manifestation of the Spirit, a Christian will be able to do things they typically will not be able to do on their own. A shy person who's been anointed by the Holy Spirit can testify about Jesus boldly and without fear. A believer undergoing persecution for being a Christian can do so with supernatural peace. This was what the apostle Paul had in mind when he wrote to the Ephesians, "I pray that he may grant you, according to the riches of his glory, to be strengthened with power in your inner being through his Spirit."*

6. The Spirit of Knowledge

The Spirit of Knowledge gives the believer the ability to know God and His thoughts in an intimate and deep way. When the Spirit of Knowledge works within a Christian, the Holy Spirit supernaturally imparts revelation of who He is and what He's seeing. It's the Holy Spirit who enables someone to encounter His love in a fresh way during worship. When a Christian prays for someone and just seems to know what to pray for, this, too, is an illumination that is given by the anointing of the Holy Spirit. Paul spoke of this in 1 Corinthians 12:8: "To one is given a message of wisdom through the Spirit, to another, a message of knowledge by the same Spirit."

7. The Spirit of the Fear of the Lord

The Spirit of the Fear of the Lord instills a profound reverence in the believer toward God's holiness and majesty. When a deep desire to please God more than people arises in you, that's from His anointing. When you feel a burning conviction to repent because of a heightened awareness of God's holiness, it's the

* Ephesians 3:16.

Spirit of the Fear of the Lord manifesting in you. It brings about a holy awakening in believers, just as it did to the church in Acts 9:31: "Living in the fear of the Lord and encouraged by the Holy Spirit, it increased in numbers."

When you survey all the ways the anointing of the Holy Spirit shows up in your life, notice how it's not limited to starting a podcast, amassing a lucrative following on social media, or becoming a respected member of your community. Although God can certainly work through these talents and accomplishments, He is far more creative and involved in every Christian's life than to be limited to those mediums. Another way to understand the anointing is this: *It is the measure of power that is personally endowed to us by the Holy Spirit to intimately set us apart to know Him and display His will and way with authority.* If you belong to Jesus, the Holy Spirit dwells in you, and He fully intends to work through you in a mighty and unique way. We do not experience this only by practicing disciplines, striving for performance, or hustling for an achievement. Instead, it's about a personal partnership with the Holy Spirit Himself.

THE HOLY SPIRIT'S PERSONALITY

Inadvertently treating the Holy Spirit as if He's just a power source can lead to religious habits that ironically lead to powerlessness. While choosing to pray more or read the Bible is always a good thing, we can often approach these practices transactionally, seeking to garner strength or favor for what we must accomplish. Anointing is not something we can earn by generating greater optimism in God's ability. Neither is it something we can strive to become worthy of. The Holy Spirit is not a gas tank that pumps fuel to our needs and dreams. Instead, *the Holy Spirit is a Divine Person to intimately know and reverently submit to.*

Acts 19:13–16 cautions against trying to wield God's power and authority without a real relationship with Him:

> Some of the itinerant Jewish exorcists also attempted to pronounce the name of the Lord Jesus over those who had evil spirits, saying, "I command you by the Jesus that Paul preaches!" Seven sons of Sceva, a Jewish high priest, were doing this. The evil spirit answered them, "I know Jesus, and I recognize Paul—but who are you?"

The sons of Sceva tried to cast out demons with the assumption that their determination and the rightful application of methods would be enough. It turns out that no matter how hard we try or how well we execute the right strategies, we will have no power against darkness unless we know Jesus—intimately, authentically, and passionately. We can't *use* the Holy Spirit, but we can partner with Him in friendship. This requires us to know Him first, to love Him for who He is, and to follow His lead.

On the day I got saved, I had a profoundly life-altering encounter with Jesus. I looked up at the stars as if my gaze could grab ahold of whatever was up there. I confessed to my Creator that I wanted to know Him—not as some idea or theory but in a deeply personal way. If having Him in my life meant that I must give my life to Jesus Christ, my Lord and Savior, then I'd do it. And then it felt as though the Holy Spirit doused me in fiery love, as if my very soul received the warmest embrace.

I wept and wept. I never felt something so peaceful and healing. It was the anointing that allowed my spiritual eyes to see the Father for who He really is. This moment marked me for life.

For a few years afterward, I wanted to revisit this moment so badly, to the point where I was frustrated by worship sessions that did not culminate with me in a pool of tears. I felt rejected when God did not show up for me in mind-blowing and sensational ways. I started to use this as an excuse to do my own thing or ignore His nearness. It wasn't until later that I realized how selfish I was being with the Holy Spirit. I wanted His perks, but I never took the time to understand Him or know Him. Instead of diving into the Bible to consider what He liked and disliked, I thought only about myself and what I wanted from Him. I reduced Him to be my mood booster instead of my Father, King, and holy Friend.

If you want to know His power, you must grow in your understanding of the Holy Spirit as a Person. Do you know what hurts Him? What delights Him? What His thoughts are? What He wants? These are the questions we would typically consider while getting to know our friends, romantic partners, and family members. Yet we so often forget to consider them for the most important relationship of our existence, our friendship with the Holy Spirit.

Here is a Scripture-based snapshot of God* as you begin to develop your personal understanding of the Holy Spirit:

* In order of appearance, please see the following scriptures: Ephesians 4:30–31; 1 Thessalonians 5:19–21; Romans 8:26–27; Acts 5:3–5; John 16:8; John 14:16; James 4:5; 1 Corinthians 12:12–13; Genesis 1:2; John 6:63; Exodus 31:1–5; Luke 3:22; Acts 1:8; Romans 5:5; Romans 8:14–16; 2 Corinthians 12:9; Acts 10:38; James 5:14–15.

- The Holy Spirit feels deep sorrow when we bitterly bad-mouth others.
- The Holy Spirit doesn't force us to listen to Him and allows us to dismiss His words.
- The Holy Spirit steps in for us when we don't know how to pray.
- The Holy Spirit is never fooled by our hypocrisy.
- The Holy Spirit is on a mission to convict people around the world of our desperate need for salvation.
- The Holy Spirit is a loyal friend.
- The Holy Spirit wants our full devotion.
- The Holy Spirit loves unity among believers.
- The Holy Spirit is creative and life-giving.
- The Holy Spirit is both powerful and gentle.
- The Holy Spirit doesn't just tell us that He loves us, but He expresses it too.
- The Holy Spirit is not impressed by self-sufficiency and independence; He's drawn to our need.
- The Holy Spirit desires to heal.

I hope this kindles your curiosity about our heavenly Friend. I'm sure you can add to this list simply by being increasingly mindful of His nearness each day. True power is found in our intimate friendship with the Holy Spirit. The anointing overflows from a deepening awareness of His presence and our growing submission to His will. We cannot steward the ministry of the Holy Spirit and be the god of our own lives. We cannot administer His power while holding on to whatever semblance of control we have over ourselves. The path to walking in God's power is to increasingly yield our own to the One we love.

If you'd like to commit (or recommit) to a journey of yieldedness to the presence and power of the Holy Spirit, pray this prayer with me:

Hello Holy Spirit,

I take this moment to make space for You and honor You. I lay down all the tricks and plays that I've been using to make things happen on my own.

I acknowledge that I need Your power. I confess that my strength and ability aren't enough.

You have been such a kind and merciful friend. You stayed with me when I went my own way. You loved me when I fell short of Your standards.

Will You help me to know You more deeply? Will You help me to be more aware of Your nearness?

In Jesus's name I pray, amen.

PAUSE AND REFLECT

1. Who is the Holy Spirit to you?
2. Are there habits, mindsets, or relationships in your life that may grieve the Holy Spirit? If you are unsure, ask Him to reveal them to you.
3. Where in your life might you be using your own power to bring about redemption, change, or healing? What would it look like to partner with the Holy Spirit instead?

5

POWER HAS A PURPOSE

I was in a coastal village of Panama with a medical team and a group of high school students. Our role was to support the medical team and minister to the children who came to play as the doctors and dentists administered care. We started one morning with a team Bible study and worship, and everyone—from the senior rheumatologist to the fourteen-year-old who knew how to make balloon animals—lifted their voices to Jesus. Our praise became petitions. Our petitions became adoration. Eventually, our team began to weep in God's presence. There was a palpable awareness of His nearness, and we experienced a deeper revelation of His compassion. One by one, we began to testify about the goodness of God and the glorious things He's done.

Later that afternoon, hundreds of locals came and stood in line to meet the doctors. While they were waiting, some of our students prayed for anyone who was willing to receive prayer.

Throughout the day, the line started to move much faster—not because the doctors were working more efficiently but because many were being healed while waiting in line. Shouts of joy erupted as cataracts disappeared in Jesus's name. Joints were freed from pain. Crutches were laid to the side as the physically impaired began to walk on their own. There was celebratory clapping and exuberant laughing.

At the end of it all, I debriefed with the team, particularly the youth, who were astounded at what God did. It was the anointing of the Holy Spirit at work in them. God had chosen those teens who were hardly entrusted with their parents' cars. He gave them authority over evil spirits and empowered them with the spiritual gift to heal! That is the purpose of the anointing—to set us apart for Himself and endow us with authority to carry out His will on earth.

OIL AND SPIRIT

To grasp the full biblical picture of anointing, we must understand the use of oil in the Old Testament. Oil was used for various purposes such as offerings, medicinal use, cosmetic reasons, oil lamps, and hospitality. In other words, it was used to worship, heal, shine light, and show favor.

Oil was also used to anoint. In the Old Testament times, anointing places, things, or people required a scented blend of oil, specially created by a perfumer, to be rubbed onto them.* This oil was used to anoint the tent of meeting, its sacred articles of worship, and the high priests—all of which were the instruments by which the people were to commune with God.

* Exodus 30:25.

So, why was oil poured and smeared onto these places, things, and people? It was to set them apart for God. Although they came from the world, they were no longer a part of it. The Holy Spirit must first make holy what He intends to use for His glory. What was once just a tent became the tent of meeting, the dwelling place for the presence of God. What was once just an altar became an instrument of worship to honor God. What was once just a human became a servant of the Most High. Oil also consecrated kings and prophets, marking them as representatives of God, entrusted with carrying out His will on earth.*

When marked with anointing oil, a person was allowed a unique connection with God, and that connection gave the person spiritual authority. Priests, kings, and prophets from the Old Testament had authority to do things for God and on behalf of God that others did not. It is the stamp of holy partnership. It wasn't the quality of the oil that made this happen. God is not oil. Yet He used (and can still use) the oil as an instrument for His presence and power.

First Samuel 16:13 recalls the moment King David was anointed with oil: "Samuel took the horn of oil and anointed him in the presence of his brothers, and the Spirit of the LORD came powerfully on David from that day forward." Notice how the oil was used to mark a person, but it was the Spirit of the Lord who gave the person power. This is why the word *anointing* isn't just about being touched by oil. It's about being touched by the Holy Spirit. This means that after Samuel anointed David with oil, the Spirit's power began working through David like never before. The anointing makes a differ-

* 1 Kings 19:15–16.

ence in us that no amount of human effort, planning, or self-discipline can. Afterward, when David worshipped around King Saul, evil spirits would flee. When he faced the giant Goliath, he had the faith and might to overcome. This was not due to the talents of a shepherd boy. It was the work of the anointing.

From the way anointing oil was used in ancient Israel, we know that the anointing of the Holy Spirit in every believer endows us with a unique connection to Him. That special access to the Divine is for every believer thanks to the indwelling of the Holy Spirit. It's not just for King David. It's not just for Elijah. It's also not just for Jesus, the "anointed one," who served as prophet, king, and priest during His ministry on earth; it's for you too. The Holy Spirit in us makes every Christian a dedicated vessel for His power. The anointing of the Holy Spirit gives you, a follower of Christ, spiritual authority like the anointed priests, kings, and prophets of the Old Testament. You don't have to helplessly watch your church break apart. You have the spiritual authority of a priest, so you can pray for them and be the bridge between heaven and despair. You don't have to watch corruption and injustice ravage your community. You have the spiritual authority of a prophet, so you can communicate God's heart. You don't have to let chaos ensue at home. You can exercise the spiritual authority of a king by making wise choices and leading your family with humility.

THE AUTHORITY FOR BREAKTHROUGH

We live in a world that covets the sort of authority that gives us the power to impress, conquer, and dominate our way forward. However, authentic kingdom victory requires spiritual authority. Spiritual authority cannot be acquired with human might and personality. Yet it's this very authority that brings about true breakthrough, and anointing equips us with it.

Let's talk about what this looks like. The Holy Spirit is the Person who dwells within us; the anointing is His power and presence that work through us. The anointing takes us from being captives of flesh and darkness to having dominion over them. It is anointing that gives us the God-given license to break off demonic oppression. It is the power of the Spirit that empowers a church greeter to encourage with authority, stirring someone who's been avoiding Jesus for decades to come back home. It's what opens the doors to places and people in need of God. It's what interrupts a heavy heart with exuberant joy. It's what moves a room full of the unamused and unmoved into a chorus of genuine praise. It's what sustains our brothers and sisters in underground churches around the world to this day, who may not have any worldly leverage but are fruitful because they have God-given authority.

The anointing empowered Peter to look at the beggar by the temple not with defeat or guilt but with confidence to say, "I don't have silver or gold, but what I do have, I give you: In the name of Jesus Christ of Nazareth, get up and walk!"* The anointing gave Paul the authority to cast out demons, shake off a deadly snake, and boldly proclaim the gospel before kings and governors, undeterred by persecution.† To have spiritual authority does not mean that we become superhuman. For example, how does a five-foot-tall teacher with a small frame command a room full of high school seniors who are bigger, louder, and stronger than she is? It's not because she's inher-

* Acts 3:6.

† Acts 16:18; 26:1–32; 28:5.

ently powerful on her own. It's because she has authority given to her by the school, and that authority grants her a measure of power. In a similar way, the anointing gives you authority from God, which grants you a measure of the Holy Spirit's power.

So, why aren't all Christians living victoriously? Even if we are well-behaved and knowledgeable believers, we can still live in ignorance of the power that dwells within. If you're not intentionally stewarding the anointing, you will live compensating for the lack of power. It may look like prioritizing performance over God's presence. You may resort to controlling instead of walking in spiritual authority. Some choose hustle over holiness. Charisma over character. People-pleasing instead of prophetic boldness. Ultimately, this will lead to burnout, whereas living anointed will keep you burning for Jesus.

Powerless Christianity may fill a calendar with good deeds and well-curated events, but it is absent of Christlike transformation, spiritual freedom, and the saving work of Jesus. A well-planned church service may gather a crowd, but it will leave the crowd the same as they came unless it also has the anointing of the Holy Spirit. We can spend years earning degrees and gaining impressive titles with still no real power to our words unless the anointing flows through us. Jesus did not die on the cross and rise again for us to become busy, well-behaved church attendees. He did not return to the right hand of the Father to send the Holy Spirit to be our babysitter to make sure we keep up with our daily devotionals and pay our tithes until we die.

When God created humanity, He gave them authority to rule over creation.* However, this God-given authority was forfeited when perfect communion with the Creator was broken

* Genesis 1:26.

by sin. This left humankind to be ravaged by shame, dysfunction, corruption, and violence. However, Christ made us children of God once again, and authority has been reinstated to us by the name of Jesus. We now have a connection to our Creator that is sealed by the Holy Spirit, and that bond restores the authority humanity once forfeited, entrusting us with God's delegated power. However, many Christians still depend on their own devices while carrying the gift of His presence. We can worship Him on Sundays while still clinging to self-sufficiency once we leave the building. You can neglect the anointing. Relying on your own strength and understanding may feel safe, but you will miss the chance to witness what He can accomplish by His power alone.

OPERATING WITH ANOINTING

When I was a newly minted pastor and working with my first youth group, I quickly found out that the job title itself did not automatically give me special abilities. My sermons were well thought out. My motivation was top-tier. I was excited to see my new young friends grow in faith. However, our Sunday worship felt like dead air. The students were unamused, despite my best efforts. There was no life. No movement. No transformation.

I realized that what I brought to the table was insufficient. Admitting this was not self-deprecating; it was simply the truth. I was trained for this job. I was in school and studying to do well at this job. However, I became painfully aware that what I longed to see happen was something only Jesus could do. Once I realized this, a hunger began to stir within me for a deeper understanding of how God works. I scoured the internet for MP3 recordings of sermons (this was before podcasts and recordings on YouTube were widespread). I visited the bookstore almost weekly, looking for books to offer some insight into what I needed. Eventually, my hunger led me to a deeper dive into Scripture and prayer.

For a time, I found myself sitting for three to four hours a day with Jesus. It wasn't piety or virtue that led me there. It was desperation, and that desperation was uncomfortable. After all, no one enjoys hunger pains. Sometimes, when I saw no visible results to my prayers, I wondered if God had abandoned me and my youth group students. Sunday after Sunday, I looked for signs that He was working. Sometimes I had no words, so I'd lie down in silence before His presence. Sometimes you could have heard me wailing in my room while worshipping. Slowly but surely, a wind started to blow through our little youth gatherings. Apathy turned to curiosity. Salvations started to happen, during service and outside the four walls of our church. I began to operate differently when I preached. Even visits with students at Starbucks felt like holy ground. I went from being a Holy Spirit carrier, living by self-reliance, to a Holy Spirit partner, intentionally operating in the anointing of the Holy Spirit.

So, how does a Christian practically operate in the anointing? Like I've said before, I generally refrain from assuming we can place a neat formula or a black-and-white system to the things of the Holy Spirit. The following is not an exhaustive to-do list that perfectly encapsulates the anointed life. However, it's a solid start.

Stir Up Spiritual Hunger

My journey began with spiritual hunger. Mind you, that doesn't always feel like a romantic longing for Jesus. Many do not feel spiritual enough because they assume spiritual hunger means you *want* to read the Bible and you *want* to pray all the time. Sometimes spiritual hunger can be a deep dissatisfaction over how things have been. It can be a frustration over your prayer life, an agitation over not being able to understand what you read in the Bible. You may find yourself asking more questions about Jesus. This all counts as spiritual hunger. To start your journey toward operating in the anointing of the Holy Spirit, you must honor this hunger by recognizing it and addressing its cries.

Psalm 42:1–2 says, "As a deer longs for flowing streams, so I long for you, God. I thirst for God, the living God. When can I come and appear before God?" These verses poetically capture the spiritual longings of the psalmist. However, have you ever been thirsty? Like *really* thirsty? It's not romantic. Extreme thirst will gnaw at you from within. You become irritable and desperate as you seek relief. It's not an inspiring experience, and yet this was how the psalmist described his spiritual hunger. Becoming a Christian who operates by the power of the Holy Spirit requires that you first acknowledge that you need Him. Today, your spiritual hunger may look like curiosity. Honor it instead of bashing it as not being spiritual enough. Or perhaps it feels like dissatisfaction. Recognize it for what it is instead of blaming people for where you are spiritually. Feed that hunger by pressing into the presence of the Lord with honest prayer, authentic praise, and meditation of Scripture.

Recommit to Your Missional Purpose

If you want to activate the anointing of the Holy Spirit in you, then you must align with what your anointing is for in the first place. The purpose of the Spirit's power is not to make us powerful but, rather, to enable us to know His greatness and display it to the world around us. Although it can bring you victory and breakthrough, the primary purpose of anointing isn't to serve *you.* It's to serve Jesus and people.

If you had no care for the souls around you to be saved, healed, and delivered by Christ, then you would not need to operate in anointing. And no, this work is not just for those who are in vocational ministry and church work; it is the mission for every believer. If you choose to neglect it, you may still have access to God's power, thanks to the blood of Christ, but you will not be intentionally drawing from it. Simply put, maybe you are not witnessing the power of the Holy Spirit in your life because you have lived as though you do not need it. Perhaps you attend Bible studies and worship services for the purpose of your own growth, comfort, and life advancement (like wanting God to show you what choices to make, whom to marry, what job to take, etc.). The anointing of the Holy Spirit is not so that you can live the life you've always dreamed of or achieve something great. Rather, it's to partner with Jesus. In Mark 16:17–18, Jesus says, "These signs will accompany those who believe: In my name they will drive out demons; they will speak in new tongues; they will pick up snakes; if they should drink anything deadly, it will not harm them; they will lay hands on the sick, and they will get well." In other words, the evidence of power is the anointing at work in a believer who dedicates their life to the sharing of the gospel to all creation.*

* Mark 16:15.

Activate Your Spiritual Gifts

The Holy Spirit equips every believer with spiritual gifts, which are God-given tools we have to engage in spiritual warfare and bless the world. How each Christian is equipped is up to the Holy Spirit. He distributes these gifts as He sees fit.* It is His will that determines who will supernaturally prophesy, serve, have a word of wisdom, and more.

If spiritual gifts are likened to tools for warfare and blessing, then the anointing of the Holy Spirit is like the batteries for these tools. How the Holy Spirit empowers you determines how effectively you use these gifts, whether it is with ease, with precision, with strength, and so on. Your anointing determines the breadth and depth of the impact you make while using your spiritual gifts. If you want to walk in God's anointing, you must not neglect the gifts the Holy Spirit has placed in you.

If you don't know what spiritual gifts to use, consider the apostle Paul's advice in 1 Corinthians 14:1: "Pursue love and desire spiritual gifts." God wants you to desire spiritual gifts, but the key is in the first part: Pursue love. If you approach every room and space with the desire to love well, then the Holy Spirit will equip you with what you need to fulfill this desire. As you love your discouraged friend, the Spirit may equip you with wisdom. As you love your sick neighbor, He may equip you with healing through your prayers. Pursue love and desire for the Holy Spirit to use you supernaturally to do just that. The Holy Spirit in you holds all the gifts. This means every Christian can be activated in any of the spiritual gifts by faith. Some may have the grace to specialize in particular gifts because

* 1 Corinthians 12:7, 11.

these show up the most frequently as they serve. Ultimately, spiritual gifts are given to us freely by grace, not by merit. However, we must intentionally partner with the Holy Spirit by seeking His guidance and relying on His empowerment as we proactively love others.

Maybe you are refraining from using your spiritual gifts out of insecurity or fear, getting caught up with thoughts like, *What if I get it wrong?* or *What if God doesn't want to use me?* In 2 Timothy 1:6–7 Paul reminded us "to rekindle the gift of God that is in you through the laying on of my hands. For God has not given us a spirit of fear, but one of power, love, and sound judgment." Paul admonished Timothy, his disciple, not to forget the anointing of the Holy Spirit. It was up to Timothy to rekindle the gift of the Spirit that had been given to him to evangelize. Notice how Paul said not "to kindle" but, rather, "to rekindle." For whatever reason, perhaps out of intimidation, Timothy began to neglect his spiritual gift. It was his responsibility to start using it again. Friend, this goes for you too. You cannot pursue love while also holding on to fear.

Before moving forward, I want to note something that Paul said to Timothy in verse 6. He mentioned that Timothy received the gift through the "laying on" of Paul's hands. Here, Paul was talking about impartation, which is the transferring of spiritual gifts and power through prayer. The act of laying on of hands is not some magical act; it is a practice of faith. Ultimately, it is God who does the impartations, but as we are His vessels, our faith partners with Him. We can see evidence of the supernatural transfer of gifts and power like this in other parts of the Bible as well.* It is essential that we recognize and

* Deuteronomy 34:9; Acts 8:17–19; Romans 1:11.

appreciate the value of a Spirit-filled community. Living out the anointed life is not meant to be done in isolation. Spiritual activation doesn't just happen as we pursue it on our own; it also happens through the sharing of lives and gifts among believers.

PAUSE AND REFLECT

1. What could pursuing love and desiring spiritual gifts look like in your day-to-day life?
2. Who around you has God called you to display His goodness to?
3. Where in your life do you need God's power? What would it look like to depend on the Holy Spirit in those areas?

6

FILLED WITH POWER

In an earlier chapter, I shared briefly about my salvation experience. I want to expand on the story a bit more here. When I was a fifteen-year-old attending a youth camp in Mexico, I made the choice to live for Jesus and love Him with all my heart. What came afterward was nothing short of a heavenly experience. A revelation of His nearness dawned on me. I realized that I was under the watchful gaze of my heavenly Father. My heart crumbled at the weight of His love, and what poured out of me was a confession, repentance, and a plea—*don't ever leave me, Jesus.* I kept repeating it: "Please don't leave me, Jesus. Please don't ever leave me." In the background, the missionary pastor grabbed a guitar and began to strum. He wasn't plugged into the speakers, nor was this a planned part of the evening program. With his worn but warm voice, he gently sang "As the Deer."

When we got to the portion of the song that says "You alone

are my strength, my shield. To you alone may my spirit yield," I felt a strange heat all over me, from the top of my head to the bottom of my feet. I wept uncontrollably. It wasn't out of sorrow; it was my reaction to being overwhelmed by this supernatural love. My spirit drank its first cup of cold, refreshing living water. It quenched all my heart's cravings—every bit of greed, pride, and lust for this world. We sang for hours in that church sanctuary, and it wasn't boring at all. My heart kept swelling with heavenly contentment. I think all of us in that room could have gone on for longer, if it hadn't been two in the morning. For the rest of that trip, I felt like there was something on me that made me more passionate when I talked about Jesus and more compassionate when I prayed for people. Believing Jesus was a no-brainer. Trusting Him felt like an honor.

I thought everything was a done deal after this experience—that I'd never struggle with sin and that I'd feel supercharged with faith for the rest of my days. But after returning home from camp, I was shocked to realize how fleeting my experience was. My palate for the world and all its ego boosting and gluttony endorsing slowly but surely returned. After some time, I wondered why even opening the Bible felt like a struggle, when just a few weeks prior, I had been fervently praying for people and sharing my testimony to anyone who would listen. I cloaked myself with shame as I did before I got saved. I did not know then what I understand now, which is that the Holy Spirit never left me after I left camp. In fact, He was with me the whole time, even through the disappointment and doubts. I simply needed to understand what it meant to be continuously filled with His power.

To cultivate a richly anointed life, every Christian must be sealed, baptized, and filled with the Holy Spirit. If you've never heard these words before, it may feel overwhelming at first. But hang tight because they will offer some context to where you are in your faith journey with Christ. Also, like I've said before, this way of wording different Holy Spirit experiences is not a cookie-cutter formula that you can plug in to make all things make sense. The tradition that you come from may use these words slightly differently. And some of these experiences can happen at the same time, so it's not exactly a step-by-step process that you have to follow. Let's dive in, shall we?

SEALED

It starts with salvation. Your salvation is not just a nominal transaction between you and your Creator that started with a "repeat after me" prayer in return for a ticket to heaven. Your acceptance of His words, your confession of your need for forgiveness, and the choice to submit to Jesus are more than a religious tradition. It's a choice that invites the Holy Spirit to take residence in you, and the power of His presence is what regenerates your dead spirit to a living one. You are not a once-pagan who is now an inspired churchgoer. The Holy Spirit doesn't just change what you do; He changes who you are into a child of God.

You become sealed with the Holy Spirit at the moment of your salvation. Ephesians 1:13 says, "In him you also were sealed with the promised Holy Spirit when you heard the word of truth, the gospel of your salvation, and when you believed." The contextual meaning for "sealed" here refers to the way owners branded their property, such as livestock or a document, as an external sign and verification of their ownership.* In other words, you're God's now. Jesus claims you as His own forever. Having the Holy Spirit does not mean you are without flaw and immune to mistakes; it simply means that you're not alone in your imperfection and that there's a relationship with God that keeps your faith alive—even if, at times, that faith is but a flicker.

I remember during my youth-pastor years, when one of my students (we'll call him Eric) finally decided he wanted to become a Christian. It was a yearlong journey for him, and he initially joined the youth group because he was lonely. For months, Eric would sit through Sunday worship and listen to sermons. He enjoyed Friday game nights and even began hanging out with church kids outside of Sunday services. One summer afternoon, he invited the pastors and mentors of the youth group to his home for lunch. He shared that he was ready to make his decision and welcome Jesus as the Lord and Savior of his life. We sat on the floor and guided him through prayer. The beauty in that moment was not in the eloquence of our words but, rather, in his newly budded faith. His eyes were clenched, and his hands were tightly clasped. It was his most earnest way of showing Jesus that he really meant what he was saying. Afterward, Eric opened his eyes and beamed. "Wow," he said. We celebrated and shared hugs, and then we spent the afternoon processing what a life with Jesus was meant to look like. There was no hype. No cameras. No publicity. Just a new son joining the Father's family and being sealed by the Holy Spirit.

If you are a believer who walks with the Holy Spirit but are

* Andrew T. Lincoln, *Ephesians*, vol. 42, Word Biblical Commentary (Word, 1990), 39.

wondering if you've ever had a "sealing experience," fear not. I've witnessed countless people whose turning point toward Jesus was not dramatic or hyperemotional. You may not have shed a tear or had any mystical encounter. Your choice to follow Jesus could have been a simple culmination of a long, gradual process. It could have been a quiet response to a holy nudge that you sensed was right. Do these count as being sealed by the Holy Spirit as well? Yes, because you heard the word of truth and you believed. The work of regenerating your spirit afterward is the Spirit's work. The transformation from stranger to God's child is accomplished by His power.

BAPTIZED

The seal of the Holy Spirit occurs when He begins to dwell within you. The baptism of the Holy Spirit occurs when the Spirit comes on you. Stick with me here.

First, the disciples came to believe the Resurrection when Jesus showed Himself to them while they were hiding in a locked room. Upon seeing His scars, they rejoiced and believed. In this moment, Jesus spoke peace and "breathed on them and said, 'Receive the Holy Spirit.'"* They were sealed by the Holy Spirit, regenerated by His presence to be sons and daughters of God. From that point, their bodies became temples of the Holy Spirit.

Next, these newly believing temples of the Holy Spirit were told to wait in Jerusalem, "for John baptized with water, but you will be baptized with the Holy Spirit in a few days."† But wait,

* John 20:22.
† Acts 1:5.

didn't the believers already have the Holy Spirit? Yes, the Holy Spirit was already in them, but Jesus was speaking about a different sort of experience here. In Acts 1:8, He said, "You will receive power when the Holy Spirit has *come on* you, and you will be my witnesses in Jerusalem, in all Judea and Samaria, and to the ends of the earth." The key words here are "come on," which in Greek is *epi*. This is when the Holy Spirit's power comes on a person, empowering them for their God-given mission.

This is a supernatural event that anoints you for your calling on earth. It could be as simple as coming away with a fresh confidence and desire to share what Jesus has done for you. Some may feel a swell of peace or joy when getting baptized by the Holy Spirit. Others may experience heat, electricity, or a weight come on them. Some may even weep while experiencing His supernatural love. There are also those who start speaking in spiritual tongues. Regardless of your experience, it's important that you don't start comparing your experience to others, measuring the worth of what God has given you to what others seem to have received from Him. Don't compare; just receive and rejoice. Just like the moment of being sealed by the Holy Spirit can come without an outward spectacle, so, too, the baptism. Also, it is quite possible for the baptism of the Holy Spirit to happen at your salvation experience. In other words, it's possible to be sealed and baptized by the Holy Spirit at the same time!

How do you know if you've been baptized by the Holy Spirit? If you are unsure, you may be tempted to backtrack to all the spiritual experiences you have had, wondering if it was epic enough to prove whether you've been baptized. However, what proves a baptism of the Holy Spirit is not the intensity of the experience in the moment but, rather, the fruit that you produce afterward. It is not a question of whether or not you cried or shook in His presence. Instead, the real metric for authenticity is this: Did something change afterward? Did you sense a deeper love for Jesus? Did you have greater courage to obey? Did you sense a new power to witness and serve Him?

Jesus specifically commanded the disciples to wait for this event. To tarry for it. These newly minted believers were now missionaries, but a mission statement was not enough for them to start the work. They had to prioritize the baptism of the Holy Spirit over productivity for the kingdom. This is the part of the account that some prefer to avoid because there's mystery in the mystical.

The baptism of the Holy Spirit is not just a fiery experience that qualifies the believer. Remember, *you already have the Holy Spirit* once you are a follower of Christ. It's a friendship that was gifted to you the moment you went from orphan to heir. This is not a game where you earn another level of salvation. Instead, the baptism of the Holy Spirit is when a Christian is fully immersed in the presence and power of the Holy Spirit for the purpose of being His witness. Salvation regenerates you to become spiritually alive; the baptism of the Holy Spirit empowers you to live like Jesus and do the works He did. Some churches hold to the belief that you get sealed and baptized at the same time, which is possible. My own salvation experience was just that—a sealing and baptism in one. However, the Bible also recounts those who were saved but needed a baptism thereafter. For example, in Acts 8:15–17, the Samaritans were already baptized in the name of Jesus but had yet to have the Holy Spirit come on them. This changed when Peter and John came to pray for them.

I encourage you not to get lost in the technicalities. The point is this: *Jesus does not just save you; He wants to empower and equip you as well.* He doesn't just rescue you; He gives you authority. Don't be afraid to want this activation, because Jesus wants every believer to have it. Christ did not suffer so that we could gatekeep grace. It is meant to overflow through us with power. It is meant to impact your family. It is meant to shake up your neighborhood, to bless and revive your church. It is meant to bring restoration to our unhoused neighbors and hope to our friends with special needs. It is meant to flood through hospital corridors and shine light in the darkest corners of the globe.

How do you get baptized by the Holy Spirit? You hunger and ask Jesus for it. Don't be afraid of the silence that envelops you when you whisper the ask. Don't interpret the stillness as God's rejection. After Jesus tasked His followers to wait for the baptism of the Holy Spirit, they lingered in an upper room to pray and wait. This is only possible if we trust what Jesus said in Luke 11:13: "If you then, who are evil, know how to give good gifts to your children, how much more will the heavenly Father give the Holy Spirit to those who ask him?"

Ask and expect Him to be a good Father to you. It can happen while you're alone in your room or while you're parked at Costco. It's not the environment that sets you up for the baptism of the Spirit. Instead, it's your spiritual hunger and the faith to ask. It can also happen through the prayers of other Christians. I've witnessed this in a living room on a Friday night, at a hangout on a beach, and during a prayer gathering at church.

One Sunday, a new face showed up at our church when we were teaching about the Holy Spirit. Although she wasn't a member of our congregation, she asked for prayer after service was over, and we stood together to pray in the corner of the sanctuary. I said a simple prayer: "Jesus, we are so grateful for You. Please baptize my new friend here by Your Holy Spirit." We quietly stood together in His presence. A minute passed (which can feel like a lifetime if you are standing quietly with someone you just met). Then another minute. Then tears began streaming down her face. After a time, she opened her eyes with her face aglow and proclaimed, "I really didn't expect this today." She was taken aback by the goodness of our Father and by realizing that all she had to do was hunger and ask.

Nevertheless, it doesn't end there. One refreshing swig of cold water from a tall glass isn't enough to keep you going for the rest of your life. Another way to describe the baptism of the Holy Spirit is to be filled by Him. Acts 2:4 recounts what took place on Pentecost in an upper room: "They were all filled with the Holy Spirit and began to speak in different tongues, as the Spirit enabled them." This was a manifestation of the baptism of the Holy Spirit, and the filling by the Holy Spirit is mentioned again and again throughout the book of Acts. So, yes, Jesus said the Holy Spirit will *come on* the believers (see Acts 1:8) while at the same time, during the event of the baptism, they were also getting *filled* with the Holy Spirit.

This is why some traditions and churches consider the filling and baptism the same thing, and they speak of the filling by the Holy Spirit as if it's a rebaptism—aka "baptized by the Holy Spirit again." Others consider baptism its own once-in-a-lifetime empowering event, where you spend the rest of your faith journey choosing to be continually filled by the Holy Spirit. Regardless, we shouldn't get too lost in the semantics, or we will find ourselves missing the point, which is that we must continuously depend on the Holy Spirit's power. After the baptism of the Holy Spirit, we must live a life that is continually getting filled by His presence.

FILLED

I want to allow some space to discuss what it means to be filled, since I believe it can be considered a uniquely separate experience. Jesus called the disciples to wait for the specific event of the baptism of the Holy Spirit so that they could be launched into the mission at hand. However, the filling came again and again as they continued in this mission, making it more like a replenishment and an ongoing empowerment. In Ephesians 5:18, Paul said to the Christians, "Don't get drunk with wine, which leads to reckless living, but *be filled* by the Spirit." This is packed with practical implications for you and me. For one, Paul was directing Christians to make a choice. If you have ever experienced or witnessed anyone being drunk off any sort of alcohol, you know what it looks like to have judgment and behavior being controlled by a substance. The experience of being filled by the Spirit is used comparatively to being drunk! However, being filled with the Spirit does not make you a more carnal version of yourself. Instead, it transforms you into a more Christlike version of yourself! It releases in you the fruit of the Spirit (love, joy, peace, patience, kindness, goodness, faithfulness, gentleness, and self-control), spiritual gifts, anointing . . . all of it!

This is great news because it means all that good stuff doesn't come from me or you! It's not up to us to fake it until we make it. We cannot conjure up joy by our own strength. We cannot love that extremely judgmental church member on our own. We cannot bring our neighbor to Christ with our experiences alone. We cannot prophesy amid conflict with only good intentions. We *must* be filled by the Holy Spirit!

To "be filled" in this verse is written as an imperative in the present tense in the original Greek language, meaning it is meant to be a continual reality and not a one-time event.* This is something you must regularly seek. There must be rhythms of freshly drinking from the well of His presence in your life. Just because you had a great experience with Jesus during that one Sunday service last month doesn't mean you don't go to Him in prayer the next day. We can't afford not to be filled by the Holy Spirit. We need His power daily.

Let's explore some ways we can be continuously filled by the Spirit.

Carry Out Your Missional Assignment with Bold Faith

When you live courageously for Jesus and dedicate your life to what He cares about on this earth, the Holy Spirit will fill you to do what only He can do. When Peter stood in front of the rulers, elders, and scribes to testify about Jesus, he became filled with the Holy Spirit.† When Stephen, the first martyr for Jesus, was being persecuted, he was full of the Holy Spirit.‡ When Paul and Barnabas got expelled by the people at Pisidian Antioch, they were filled with joy and the Holy Spirit.§ In all of these cases, Christians were obeying the Holy Spirit and sharing the gospel. If you are living by bold faith, the Holy Spirit will not leave you hanging out to dry; He will give you the

* Andrew T. Lincoln, *Ephesians*, vol. 42, Word Biblical Commentary (Word, 1990), 344.

† Acts 4:8.

‡ Acts 7:55.

§ Acts 13:52.

confidence you need to face opposition. He will fill you with delight in the face of rejection. When you show up for His name and glory, He will meet you where you are by filling you with His power. What is your missional assignment right now? Is it to testify about your faith to your grandmother who hates the church? Is it to invite your longtime friend to worship with you this Sunday? Is it to stand up for the student Christian club at the school you work in?

Fervently Pray and Commune with the Holy Spirit

After Peter and John were released from jail, they reported to their community all the threats they had received from the Jewish leadership. What did the community do? They *fervently prayed,* and the place where they assembled shook. They received a fresh filling of the Holy Spirit!* However, intentional communion with the Spirit is not limited to prayer. You can also commune with the Holy Spirit by meditating on Scripture. The apostle Paul said in Colossians 3:16, "Let the word of Christ dwell richly among you, in all wisdom teaching and admonishing one another through psalms, hymns, and spiritual songs, singing to God with gratitude in your hearts."† Linger in His presence. Praise Him for all the good you see Him doing. Cry out to Him amid your troubles. Even when there are no fireworks to your prayers, lean in. The silence is not an absence of

* See Acts 4:23–31.

† What's described here looks very similar to when Paul told the Ephesians not to get drunk on wine but be filled with the Spirit. He described in Ephesians 5:19–21 what being filled in the Spirit looks like, which is "speaking to one another in psalms, hymns, and spiritual songs, singing and making music with your heart to the Lord, giving thanks always for everything to God the Father in the name of our Lord Jesus Christ, submitting to one another in the fear of Christ."

His presence. The anointing flows from your continual communion with the Holy Spirit.

Some of these practices may not be new to you. Perhaps you hoped that I would offer some revolutionary tactic that would radically change your life. You may *be* praying. You may *be* taking all the big risks for Jesus and still feeling empty. Let me tell you—I've been there.

There is no perfect formula that will allow you to bypass the beautiful mystery and steady pace of partnering with the Holy Spirit. It's not *just* prayer. It's not *just* meditating on Scripture. It's not *just* silently lingering in His presence. Your physical senses may pester you about wasting your time as if nothing is happening. After all, even the sight of fire and cloud through the wilderness became ordinary and uneventful to the Israelites. We do that as humans. We don't see the worth of what's happening unless it's something we've never seen before. Unless it wows us and blows us away. In 2022, Lumen Research revealed that it takes approximately 1.7 seconds for someone to scroll past a Facebook video ad.* We live in an age when corporations are spending millions to research and strategize how to attain and retain your attention so that you deem what they sell worthwhile. Every time we see a billboard, watch a commercial, or scroll through social media, we are being pushed and pulled by the latest attention-grabbing image or sound. But God doesn't play that game. He isn't going to clickbait you into living an anointed Christian life!

* "Attention Comes of Age," Lumen Research, January 31, 2022, https://lumen-research.com/blog/attention-comes-of-age.

You can be saved and still be stagnant. Called while living powerlessly. Once baptized by the Holy Spirit but leaking oil now. The followers of Christ in the upper room had an unprecedented experience with the fire of the Holy Spirit at Pentecost. And then they experienced it again and again and again. The first touch from God isn't the final one. To be everyday, anointed Christians who walk in power and authority, we must also remain needy with the Holy Spirit. We may have experienced a wondrous encounter with His heavenly love before. We just need it again. And again.

PAUSE AND REFLECT

1. What stage of the spiritual journey should you be leaning into—being sealed, baptized, or filled?
2. What would it look like for you to prioritize the filling of the Holy Spirit?
3. What would change if you were fully convinced that being sealed by the Holy Spirit is the truest aspect of your identity?

7

GROW IN POWER

If you've ever been in Christian spaces where *anointing* is a part of the everyday language, you may have heard these statements:

- "Wow, he is so anointed!"
- "The anointing is all over her."
- "That time of worship was so anointed."
- "The anointing is here."

Unintentionally, this can leave some of us thinking that the anointing is an elusive power that comes and goes and something only a few uniquely gifted people possess. But Scripture tells a different story. The anointing of the Holy Spirit is not only in every believer but is meant to grow as well. That doesn't mean you receive more of the Spirit—He's already given

Himself to you in fullness.* However, when we become more yielded, available, and aligned with His purposes, we experience a greater measure of His power. David was anointed three times, each marking an increase in responsibility and authority, before he fully assumed his role as king of God's people.† Elisha boldly requested a double portion of the anointing that rested on Elijah, and he received a larger portion of the Spirit's power.‡ Even Jesus, who is perfect and sinless, went into the wilderness filled with the Holy Spirit and left the wilderness in power.§ Soon after, He entered the synagogue to read from Isaiah 61: "The Spirit of the Lord is on me, because he has anointed me."¶

Every Christian has the anointing of the Holy Spirit, but it doesn't just end with possession. It's not like that expensive sweater that's stored in the back of the closet only to be used on special occasions. We are to regularly steward the anointing and experience its *increase* over our lives. It's not about receiving "more" of the Holy Spirit as if He comes in parts but, rather, about increasing how much we access His power. Although the Spirit is given to us fully, our experience and expression of His power can increase.

A LOUDER YES

Once I realized that the key to seeing souls transformed and neighborhoods renewed was the anointing of the Holy Spirit, I

* Colossians 2:9–10.

† 1 Samuel 16; 2 Samuel 2; 2 Samuel 5.

‡ 2 Kings 2:9.

§ Luke 4:1,14.

¶ Luke 4:18.

searched for understanding. I wanted to learn how to attain what seemed like a heavenly entity and wield its effects. I spent whatever I had left from my paycheck as a youth pastor to buy books that offered any insight into how to take hold of this power and use it for good. I watched documentaries about revivals. I studied the lives of anointed preachers and missionaries. Ultimately, I realized that the power of the Holy Spirit was never meant to be harnessed and controlled. We are stewards, not owners. We are children of God, not clients who can buy power in exchange for piety.

There was one through line, though, one common practice that was shared among all the people, movements, and events I studied. There was always *prayer*. I'll be honest, this was the most dissatisfactory finding for me, and I spent years trying to find alternative means and methods. I was sure there had to be a secret key to discover, an uncommon revelation to attain. I could not wrap my head around how ordinary it was. Just pray? So, if I added another hour to my prayer times, would I be able to do more for God? Was that it?

When Jesus came down from the mountain alongside Peter, James, and John, they were immediately faced with a spectacle. Now, mind you, just moments before, they had stood in glory—literally. On the mountaintop, Jesus was transfigured before their very eyes, radiating divine light, and they witnessed the spirits of Elijah and Moses talking to Jesus. What a sight! What an encounter! It was holy and otherworldly. Yet the moment they arrived at ground level, they faced the reality of life: desperation and disorder. A problem that could not be solved simply with good intentions and strong will. A boy who was seized by a demonic spirit was brought before Jesus's disciples, and they could not cast it out. They tried but failed. The crowd was agitated. The religious scribes hurled accusations. Then Jesus simply rebuked the demon from the child and went into the privacy of a home with the disciples.

They asked Him, "Why couldn't we drive it out?"*

Isn't that always the question? We ask similar ones: Why wasn't he healed when I prayed for him? Why isn't my family changing after years of intercession? Why don't my words of encouragement have impact? Why does it feel like demons follow me instead of flee from me? Where's the victory, Lord? Where's the breakthrough? If the architect of the cosmos and the sustainer of all things resides in me, surely, I'd have the power to at least hold my tongue when someone offends me!

Sometimes, it is simply that Jesus is doing something behind the scenes that we cannot perceive just yet. Other times, however, we need to live by the authority that's been placed in us by the Holy Spirit in greater measure.

Jesus responded, "This kind can come out by nothing but prayer."† Let's start with those words "this kind," which insinuate that there are different kinds of opposition, some of which require a deeper faith that allows us to fully steward the authority delegated to us. In other words, the disciples needed to access a greater measure of God's power for this spiritual battle, and the key to meeting this need comes from the intimacy of prayer.

Jesus is not talking about prayer and fasting as if they are events, like an item to scratch off your checklist. He's referring to a heightened dedication to intimacy with the Holy Spirit. A lifestyle of prayer and fasting looks foolish to the world around

* Mark 9:28.

† Mark 9:29.

us, but the ones who make the investment will experience its heavenly returns. To pause productivity to sit with an invisible King will not always feel like the best use of time. To withhold our favorite foods to soften our hearts to His leading looks sadistic to others who do not know Jesus. It takes great faith to make sacrifices of time and comfort so that our friendship with God can gain. However, isn't this a no-brainer for any relationship of value? The anointing gets weightier and heightens spiritual authority when our friendship with the Holy Spirit deepens. It's not just about giving Him more time. It's about a greater yieldedness. A heart bowed lower. A louder yes to His will and way.

There came a point in my growing ministry work when I knew I needed extra administrative help. I couldn't respond to every email or arrange every meeting on my own, so I went on a long quest to find a person I could partner with. Soon, I met someone who was perfect for the job. How did I know she was the one? She took the time to get to know me. She asked questions and carefully listened to my answers. She wanted to understand my mission, my life goals, and my everyday challenges. I later had no problem having her represent me in conversations and talk to others on my behalf. Why? I knew that she would communicate my intentions, tone, and goals in a way that accurately represented who I am. The more we were aligned, the more I entrusted to her.

A life doused in prayer and fasting is one that is increasingly aligned with the heart of God. When we are in communion with our King, the growing connectedness will empower us to entrust Him with our will and ambition. It begins with a yes to a conversation with the Holy Spirit, but as the conversation continues and the sacred connection grows, that yes becomes louder. We give in to love. Eventually, it's not just a yes to the prayer time. It's also . . .

Yes to His timing.
Yes to His mission.
Yes to His way.
Yes to forgiveness.
Yes to serving others.
Yes to loving the unlovable.
Yes to the interruptions.
A louder YES.

YIELDING TO TRANSFORMATION

To host a greater measure of God's power, we must be impacted by that power as well. The anointing cannot continuously and increasingly flow through us if we are not being transformed by it first. We discern the level someone is accessing their God-given spiritual authority by how Christlike they are—how undone and redone they've become by His love. This isn't about what someone does on the weekends. I'm speaking of someone's *Christlikeness,* how they think like Jesus and embody His heart.

One of the most anointed people I've known is someone who's gone home to be with the Lord. He was a professor of leadership development at a seminary I attended. He and a team of professors gave a workshop on soul care and inner healing. The Holy Spirit was the center of attention all weekend. After every teaching, we were led through a time of corporate prayer that left us freer every time. Deep soul wounds were healed. Demonic oppression was cast away. Secrets turned into testimonies. It was heavenly. During one of the breaks, I ran into this particular professor, but being that he was avidly sought after throughout the conference, I greeted him and started to move on. Yet he didn't move on. Unhurried, he asked me how I was doing, what I was learning, what God was doing in my life. He took the time to listen. We even had time for some jokes and laughs. I'll never forget how his grandfatherly eyes teared up when I told him what God was doing in me. I felt the compassion of Christ through him. Then he proceeded to encourage me, very intentionally so. He started to tell me what he saw in me, and he included details that only God would know. Nevertheless, it was his kindness that marked me, his gentle shepherding presence that imitated the very essence of our Good Shepherd. When I walked away, I wasn't amazed at how gifted he was. Instead, I was moved by how good God is.

We don't become more anointed by being more educated and experienced. It doesn't increase with more church events under our belt. More anointing doesn't come on us when we attain a thousand more followers on social media. It's not when people start to recognize our calling or when the opportunities roll in. It's not when someone chooses us for a position or role in the church. Even attaining our family goals, whether it is marriage or children, doesn't add more power to our lives. Ironically, we think these are the kind of things that will make us more useful to Jesus. In fact, it's when we cultivate a genuine friendship with Jesus and submit to the inevitable pruning process of abiding in His presence. However, when we resist this process, we accept a powerless Christianity that may appear devout but has no effect against darkness.

That's what happened to King Saul (remember him?). After

the prophet Samuel poured oil on Saul, God anointed him to prophesy and lead.* A man who once trembled behind a pile of supplies now had the ability to rule on behalf of God, and it was God who enabled him to do so. Yet Saul persisted in being prideful, disobedient, controlling, unteachable, and bitter. Eventually, his kingship prematurely ended. Contrast this with King David, whom the prophet Samuel also anointed with oil. David also had an extensive list of wrongdoings. He committed adultery, orchestrated a murder, lied . . . just to name a few. However, when God confronted David with the reality of his faults, David always admitted, "I have sinned."† Ultimately, Saul was crushed by the weight of the anointing because he refused to bend to it, whereas David's throne was established forever through Jesus Christ.

We can learn from the way Saul remained unteachable to the anointing on his life. We, too, can be unyielding to the Holy Spirit's transformative power. The following is how that might look.

Feeling Entitled to God's Helping Hand

If you feel that your sacrifice, suffering, and service merit a more powerful move of God, you are likely frustrated or let down when it seems like they amount to nothing. Have you prayed for years with lackluster results? Entitlement will tempt you to quit praying altogether. Have you served at a church ministry and given it your best, only to be unappreciated at the end? Entitlement will tell you it was a waste of time. Saul was a steward of God's power, but he started taking things into his

* 1 Samuel 10:1–10; 11:6.

† 2 Samuel 12:13; 24:10.

own hands when God's power did not move the way he wanted it to. If you find yourself relating to this, then you have the opportunity now to sacrifice, endure, and serve simply because Jesus is worthy—not because the results are desirable.

Valuing the Fruit of His Power More Than His Presence

The anointing gives you results, and it feels good. It opens doors. Bodies and souls get healed. People are delivered from the bondage of fear and shame. They begin to produce the peace, love, and joy that come only from God Himself. This is merely a small picture of what the anointing does in one's life. It can be thrilling to witness—and it can stir up an appetite for miracles, breakthroughs, and more blessings. As children of God, there is no fault in loving what God does. In fact, we are given permission to ask for these things. The problem is when we pursue the effects of the anointing more than the One who anoints. When we fall into this trap, we no longer devote ourselves to God, but rather, we devote ourselves to what we want from God.

Elevating Oneself over Others

The Holy Spirit does not anoint us so that we can become great. On the contrary, He empowers us to reflect His greatness. Even so, it is possible to mistake the things we do by His power as the result of our own hustle, talent, or piety. Yet here's the truth: Our pride has no place before God. The Spirit of Wisdom may have helped you make the right financial moves to expand your business, and yet you can drift into the belief that it was because of your genius strategies. You may have felt led by the Spirit to host a modest Bible study in your living room that eventually burgeoned into a full-blown ministry, but at some point, you begin to take credit for its growth. Those who adopt a "this is how I did it" attitude start inviting people to give credit to their means and methods more than steering them toward the Holy Spirit. God challenged Saul's pride by elevating David, and instead of humbling himself, Saul fought to maintain his status. Is the Holy Spirit challenging your ego in any way? Don't fight it. Let the ego die.

Fearing People More Than God

To be a faithful steward of God's power, we must forfeit the approval of people. The Achilles' heel to Saul's leadership was his paralyzing fear of people's opinions. It drove him to act out of people-pleasing rather than obedience to God. He placed his worth on what people said of him instead of what God said of him. And although the Spirit of the Lord was on him to give him everything he needed to lead God's people, Saul let his insecurity drive him into jealousy, rage, and an obsessive need to defend his throne. If we want God's power to help us be an encouraging neighbor, a wise parent, a faithful spouse, or a God-honoring co-worker, then we need to have a healthy fear of the Lord, one that convicts us to revere God enough to obey His commands even at the risk of being misunderstood or devalued by others.

Abusing Power

God entrusted Saul with power, and he abused it. Instead of administering God's justice and mercy, Saul mistreated people. He was given authority to serve, but he used it to control and manipulate instead. He killed innocent priests for helping David, and even after that, he executed an entire town of vulnerable men, women, and children. He made rash oaths to force his hand, consequently placing his own son in danger. He pursued and persecuted David and his allies out of his own paranoia. He used people, including his own daughter, as pawns under his control. How we view and treat people, especially the vulnerable and marginalized, matters if we want to faithfully steward the anointing of the Holy Spirit. If you've paid attention to nationwide church news, then you know something about the fall of leaders and ministries that once held immense influence, some with a global reach. However, the Holy Spirit cannot be mocked. He doesn't continue to administer great power to those who continue to selfishly use power and mistreat others.

The Holy Spirit will never force you to change. He will help you, for He is the Helper, after all. He will teach you, strengthen you, and counsel you. Even so, you must still cooperate with Him and participate in your transformation. In Galatians 5:22–23, Paul wrote that the fruit of the Spirit is "love, joy, peace, patience, kindness, goodness, faithfulness, gentleness, and self-control." To produce these things, we must constantly choose to follow the Holy Spirit over the direction and desires of our flesh.

Imagine you have two friends, one who is heading to the mall and the other who is going to the beach. Following either one may seem enticing. However, whom you follow will determine what you do and gain. I'm not inferring that in real life either one would be a bad choice, but for the sake of the analogy, stay with me. If I were to tell you that you need more exercise and sunshine, you would naturally follow the friend going to the beach. In that same way, if you want to produce the fruit of the Spirit, follow the Spirit, not your compulsive desires and carnal ego. Follow Him like you would a loyal friend. Choose His path, even though others may take a more common road. Choose His holy words over your own self-condemning or judgmental thoughts. Follow His directions to go where He goes. As you do, you will experience what only He can produce in you.

To steward the anointing is a heavenly privilege granted to us by grace. We aren't entitled to it, and neither should we disregard it. We must acknowledge that we cannot earn it, that it's given to us by the kindness of Christ. Hold it like it's the most precious gift. If you must lower yourself to hold it well, so be it. If you must forgo hypocrisy to keep operating in it, may it be so. If there's prejudice in you that keeps you from administering the anointing faithfully, let repentance be the next step. You cannot expect to keep holding fire without it changing you.

POWER IN THE QUIET

A misconception that many have about the anointing of the Holy Spirit is that we will know it's there by the way we feel. On the contrary, anointing can sometimes feel unremarkable and mundane. Do not mistake the anointing as hype. It is not a feel-good drug that God grants us to feel better about life. It is not an emotional crutch to coddle our insecurities. Just because we do not see it or feel it does not mean it is not working. Walking in the anointing requires us to resist the idea that sensational feelings and extraordinary experiences are the main evidence that God is working through us.

I have a prayer partner I pray with every Wednesday morning. We talk for the first thirty minutes, sharing our prayer requests. At one time, I would persistently say "Can you pray that God will anoint me to write that Bible study?" or "Can you pray that God will anoint me to have this tough conversation with this one person?" One day my friend finally said, "Faith! You *are* anointed!" She was right. I just didn't *feel* anointed, and my preoccupation with my own weakness was keeping me from acknowledging His power in me.

When you pray for God's power to manifest through you, don't seek to feel better about yourself as proof that God's doing something. This is not a superhero movie where someone gets a super serum that amps them up to become this otherworldly version of themselves. The Holy Spirit doesn't serve your cravings for spiritual thrills and emotional highs. Remember, your walk with Christ started with faith, and it must continue with faith. We cannot take a leap of trust in the beginning and then demand emotional affirmation in every step that follows.

When we consider those who clearly carry the power of God, certain Bible stories may come to mind. Elijah called forth fire from the sky. Paul cast out demons, and even the handkerchiefs and aprons that touched his skin held healing—miraculous power. God clearly entrusted His power to these people, and they walked in a kind of spiritual authority that made them seem invincible. Of course, let us not forget that these were just a handful of scenes in the scope of their entire lives. The Holy Spirit's power may have manifested as miracles one day. But on other days? Elijah the fiery prophet also spent periods of time drinking from a brook during a drought, hiding in a widow's home and living off her modest provisions, and walking for forty days in the desert alone. As for Paul, he likely spent the first hours of the day doing manual labor and selling tents so that he could teach and preach after work. He also spent years in prison, and it doesn't take much to imagine the monotonous rhythm of each day there. But it was from his cell that Paul changed the world through his letters to the church. The anointed life does not discount you from the boring, ordinary, and mundane. God's power works there too.

Some of the most anointed people I've encountered did not lead very attention-grabbing lives. For example, the nurse in the ICU whose gentle touch embodies the compassion of Christ. The entrepreneur that quietly builds a business with spiritual insight and gives as a vessel of God's generosity toward those in need. The foster parents who build a home where every child within its walls encounters the unconditional love of their heavenly Father. The blue-collar worker who fixes pipes or drives trucks while also counseling colleagues during lunch breaks and praying for people when no one is watching. They, too, are anointed by the Holy Spirit. Just because their lives don't have brand names doesn't mean they are not breaking chains and ushering redemptive power. The anointing does not need to be dressed in fanfare and spectacle because it is pure power.

When I was sixteen years old, my parents surprised me with a brand-new car—a silver Honda Accord Coupe EX-L V6. Looking back, I'm fully aware of what a gracious and generous gift this was. But I did not know how to maintain a car and was also a very skittish driver. When I was in high school, the movie franchise *Fast & Furious* was becoming a cultural phenomenon, so many of the high schoolers in the area were obsessed with modifying their cars with custom body kits or the kind of mufflers that would roar through the streets. Teenagers became obsessed with cars. They talked about them, thought about them, saved money for them, researched them, and so on. Even on weekdays, there would be late-night meets in some obscure parking lot where they would test what their vehicles were capable of. So, when my car-enthusiast friends saw my new gift, they exploded with excitement . . . for a second. Then one of them playfully teased, "Man, we will never know what this car can do because Faith will be driving it!" I laughed because I fully understood (and agreed to) what he meant. I was going to drive this car at the speed limit, to the library and the mall, at most. No one was ever going to witness how quickly the car could reach high speeds. Or how the car could handle sharp corners and turns. Or how smoothly the car responded to the driver. To this day, I still don't know.

Some of us carry the anointing like how I drove my Honda Accord Coupe. We access it for Sunday worship and the occasional Bible study. Aside from that, we keep it tidily tucked away instead of giving it some miles and allowing it to be part of our daily lives. The Holy Spirit is often referred to as a gift in the New Testament.* Our Father in heaven paid a high price for us to carry His power. It is an unfortunate but undeniable reality that there are those who never get to witness how great God is because a Christian chooses not to fully access what's been gifted to them. So, I ask, are you growing in anointing?

* Luke 11:13; Acts 2:38; 10:44–45.

PAUSE AND REFLECT

1. Do you ever resist the Holy Spirit's transformative power? What would it look like for you to stop resisting?
2. When you are not feeling God's power, what are some of the rising thoughts and assumptions that discourage your faith?
3. What would it look like to intentionally follow the Holy Spirit and not your sinful inclinations?

LIKE CHRIST

The purpose of this final section is to take Jesus at His word when He said, "Truly I tell you, the one who believes in me will also do the works that I do. And he will do even greater works than these, because I am going to the Father."* As followers of Jesus and lovers of His presence, we are not mandated to spend the rest of our days in self-discovery and ideal-lifestyle-building. The Great Commission was not "Go and be loved, seen, and heard by those you care about." It was not "Go and build a great life and fulfill all your goals and aspirations."

Now, don't get me wrong: Having dreams for your life is a beautiful thing. From the beginning in the garden, we were created to be expanders and builders. So, please hear

* John 14:12.

me when I say, it is not selfish to have desires for your life. By default, we were made to be blessed by God. However, these blessings are to be an overflow of our alignment with Jesus. And when we align with Him, His dreams and desires are the source from which our own overflow.

So, what was Jesus's dream for us? He said, "Go, therefore, and make disciples of all nations, baptizing them in the name of the Father and of the Son and of the Holy Spirit, teaching them to observe everything I have commanded you. And remember, I am with you always, to the end of the age."*

He wants to bring people into His family, and He wants to do it with us, until the trumpets sound. How each of us aligns with Christ's dream will vary. You are the only person on earth who can shine His light in your unique way. You know that you have the anointing of the Holy Spirit. Now let's get into the details of how to use this power to glorify Jesus through each of our lives.

It's time to get practical. Each of the following chapters will end with suggested ways to activate the anointing in you. The only way to fall short is to refuse to try and to not put conviction into action!

* Matthew 28:19–20.

8

TURN WATER INTO WINE

You might not consider yourself someone who is called to do miracles. You're not alone in this. For starters, most of us are just trying to get through the week—show up to work, pay bills, keep up with chores, and such. We tend to think the business of miracles is for someone who has time for it or maybe someone who's especially chosen for it. Miracles may be shared about as someone else's testimony or read about in the Bible. But are you willing to believe that *you* can be an agent of God's power as well? In fact, everyday life with everyday problems can be the stage God chooses to display His glory. After all, that's what Jesus did at a wedding in a little place called Cana of Galilee.

This miracle didn't happen front and center for all the guests to see. It took place not among the festivities but, rather, in the preparation area where the servants were located. The setting was humble, and the audience was small.

Jesus's turning water into wine was the first of many signs that revealed He is the Messiah and Son of God. It was the thunderclap that heralded the start of His three-year ministry and His journey to the cross. It signaled that a new age was upon them. The ultimate Bridegroom had arrived, and He brought His own wine with Him. Although this was a divine sign revealing Jesus's messianic identity, it was also the way He began His three years of demonstrating what it looks like when humankind is fully yielded to the Spirit. It's the Holy Spirit who turned water into wine, the same Holy Spirit that you and I are to partner with today.

For Christians who are called to do the works that Christ does, Jesus's miracle at Cana is a personal invitation to us. And, no, this isn't a green light for you to go around crashing weddings with a bottle of Dasani and a prayer. The real water-to-wine Christian is one who doesn't underestimate what God can do in an ordinary setting with everyday need. After Jesus conducted this miracle, the disciples in His circle came to believe. Friend, this is not about us learning how to pull inspirational party tricks. Instead, this is about the faith of our neighbors, family members, and friends. God wants to glorify Jesus through your life. Yes, *your* life.

INVITE HIM INTO THE NEED

For Christians to walk in spiritual authority and be witnesses to what only the Holy Spirit can do, *faith looks like an invitation to the Holy Spirit.* An invitation is a request for one's presence. It opens the door and offers someone to take space. Now, you may be wondering, *Isn't God everywhere? Why does He need our invitation?* Yes, God is everywhere, but He is also *some-*

where. God's presence is both beyond us, greater than anything we can imagine, and right here with us, close and personal. As in, He's both transcendent and immanent, omnipresent yet relationally accessible, thanks to the saving work of Christ. As much as He is near the stars in the sky and the craters in the earth, the presence of God has always wanted to be *with you.* He ultimately bled for it. At first, He walked with humanity in the Garden of Eden, but He was rejected there. He whispered His promises to the patriarchs, who continued to lie and cheat their way through life. He shepherded His children through the wilderness by cloud and fire, despite their grumbling and blaming. He dwelled with His people in a tabernacle and then a temple, despite the idols they created and the disobedience that persisted. He spoke to us through prophets, even when no one was listening. He walked among us as Jesus, although He was unjustly shamed and persecuted. And now, by the blood of the Lamb, He dwells within you and me. So, what will we do now? Will we ignore Him or blame Him as our predecessors have done? Or will we welcome Him in and reciprocate His perpetual offer for friendship?

Yes, your invitation matters.

It starts with yielding your impossible circumstance to God and making space for Him to move accordingly. Now, Jesus was the one who turned water into wine. *God* did the miracle, and *God* will do every miracle that we get to witness in our lifetimes. Yet we also have Mary, Jesus's mother, to thank, since she nudged Him to it! She invited Him into that preparation space where the servants were and said, "They don't have any wine."* Here was a problem that could shame the hosts of the wedding

* John 2:3.

banquet, and Mary reached for Jesus. Did she know how He was going to fix the problem? Likely not. There was little reason for Jesus to be included in this predicament. It wasn't His problem to deal with. Yet she invited Him into the situation anyway.

We must be in the habit of inviting the Holy Spirit into our everyday predicaments, even when we don't know how He is going to fix the problem, meet the need, or address the issue. It's not just about giving Him permission to work in our lives; He does not need our permission. But it is an *intentional partnership.* Let's not forget: God did not come to die on the cross, resurrect, and save us so that we can be bystanders to the rest of what He does in redemptive history. Remember His dreams for us? He wants you and me to bring as many people as possible into His family, and He wants to do it *with* us. This means we must be participants, not just idle onlookers.

After my first time reading through the book of Acts as a young believer, I closed my Bible and asked the Lord, "Why did You do so much back then for the early church and so little for us?" This New Testament book depicted what seemed like a Holy Spirit party, chapter after chapter, whereas modern-day believers seem to be settling for polished worship services and learning tips and tricks on how to be happy with our lives. Admittedly, this was a very narrow-minded question because if we just put our ears to the ground and take a pulse of what is going on in the world, we will hear endless stories of what the Holy Spirit is up to today. He isn't in slumber. He didn't stop moving. Some of us simply aren't moving with Him.

After my shortsighted question, the Lord kindly challenged me with this: *Does your life have room for Me to move?* At that time, as a novice and eager believer, I tried to fill my life to the brim with good things. I was going to Bible studies and had Christian radio on whenever I drove. I went to church gatherings and wore youth camp shirts to school. Yet this gentle challenge from the Holy Spirit shed light on the fact that none of what I was doing required much faith. Of course, it wasn't a waste of time, because all these activities were beneficial in some way to my spiritual growth. However, I rarely paused to invite Him to move in a way I could not by my own strength. I was great at participating in Christian events, but I was not proactively and intentionally partnering with the Holy Spirit.

If inviting Jesus into your everyday needs is not something you do on a regular basis, there may be some assumptions keeping you from taking that step of faith. Here are some common ones:

- *This is too trivial and small to bother involving Him.* We do not need to reserve our invitations for only the "big" problems in life. Asking Jesus to help isn't just for emergencies; it's also for awkward moments and minor roadblocks. We cannot make that assumption for Jesus. When we let this hinder us, we decide for Him whether He should be involved or not. Invite Him anyway and let Him reveal Himself to you according to His will and way. The predicament at the wedding at Cana wasn't a life-or-death problem. No one was in grave danger. This wasn't a war or famine. Running out of wine at a wedding party was simply a social faux pas that would have brought shame to the hosts, and yet Jesus said yes to the invitation.
- *He won't care.* Again with the assumptions! Does it not say in 1 Peter 5:7 that we should cast all our anxieties on

Him because He cares for us? When we assume God's lack of care, we become our own obstacle by leaving Him out of the details. At the wedding in Cana, instead of wondering whether Jesus would be interested in getting involved or not, Mary included Him anyway.

- *I cannot imagine what He could possibly do about this problem.* There have been several times when I simply did not pray about a circumstance because I did not know what to suggest for Him to do! I couldn't imagine what He could possibly do, so I defaulted to autopilot instead of handing Him the controls. There is no indication in this story that Jesus had been in the business of turning water into wine before this miracle at the wedding. One can assume that this was not a regular occurrence and likely unprecedented. So, did Mary know exactly what Jesus was going to do to solve this problem? Probably not. Yet she still invited Him to address the matter and do it the way He saw fit.

George Müller was an evangelist during the 1800s in Bristol, England, and he dedicated his life to protecting orphans and raising them in the faith. At one point, he housed three hundred children, and they all woke up one morning to no food available in the kitchen. As his staff scurried in a panic, Müller directed the children to get dressed for school and get seated at the table. He could have succumbed to panic himself. He could have become bitter over the burden of his calling. Yet he gathered the children and staff to give thanks, inviting Jehovah Jireh, the God who Provides, to the empty table. Only moments later, a baker came knocking with fresh bread in his arms. Then, minutes later, a milkman's cart broke down just outside the orphanage, leaving the children with free milk since the milkman would not be able to fix the cart in time to deliver the milk before it spoiled.* Who knew how the Holy Spirit was going to feed these children! All Müller had to do was invite Jesus into that dining room the morning before school, and God took up his invitation.

DO WHATEVER HE TELLS YOU

> "Do whatever he tells you," his mother told the servants.†

These simple words unveil the key to partnering with the Holy Spirit and having a front-row seat to His glory on display. *Just do whatever He tells you.* The pathway toward spiritual breakthrough is in what He says, whether it be through Scripture or during prayer. You will not witness healing in your family simply by trying to be a good person. Religious striving will not attain the divine protection over your car as you travel cross-country or supernatural provision for your student loans. Optimism will not revive our churches. Sacrifice alone will not change the unbeliever's mind.

Human beings cannot fabricate redemption by their own strength. We experience it by following Jesus and obeying His words. The formula for the Holy Spirit's miracles is in His direction. The power doesn't come from us, so it's not a matter of what we're able to do or what plan we can think of. Instead, it's a matter of what He's telling us to do. What does Scripture say? What are the Holy Spirit's marching orders for us amid the challenge? God's power is shared with us as a gift, not as a

* Roger Steer, *George Müller: Delighted in God* (Harold Shaw, 1981), 131.

† John 2:5.

reward for our abilities and fortitude. Often when the Holy Spirit's power is mentioned in the Bible, grace is mentioned as well. For example:

> With great *power* the apostles were giving testimony to the resurrection of the Lord Jesus, and great *grace* was on all of them.*

> Stephen, full of *grace* and *power,* was performing great wonders and signs among the people.†

> [The Lord] said to [Paul], "My *grace* is sufficient for you, for my *power* is perfected in weakness."‡

How do we tap into this undeserved grace? Again, by doing whatever He tells us to do. So, the question is not "What will it take to fix this?" or "How can I make this happen?" Instead, it's "What does Jesus say?"

As I've shared already, when my family and I were church planting in 2020, we were thrown into a whirlwind of unexpected and confusing challenges. We weren't anticipating building a team amid a statewide lockdown. We didn't know we would be trying to gather for worship with no available indoor public spaces in our vicinity. Very rapidly, we found ourselves with no worship space, no team, no funding, and no direction. On top of all this, my family of six was living in a home where our agreement would run its course by the end of June. My husband and I were lost as to what to do. We couldn't go house

* Acts 4:33.
† Acts 6:8.
‡ 2 Corinthians 12:9.

hunting during the lockdown. At the same time, we were living off our limited savings account. Each day that passed made waking up to a new one a little heavier. It was a pressing situation, and we were desperate for solutions. What started out as a God-given dream for northern New Jersey ended up being a game of survival.

At first, our prayers were, "Lord, give us a home to move into!" Every time I prayed those words, I faced the dread of silence. It was extremely uncomfortable to sit in the unknown for what felt like forever. I felt as though I needed to take things into my own hands because it seemed like I cared more about the situation than God did. My mind would race for something, *anything,* I could do to get unstuck from my predicament. I began to wonder if we simply weren't supposed to fix this by our own means. Then my husband came out of his prayer corner and said, "The Lord told us to do nothing. Do not look for a house until the end of May." *End of May?* I was aghast. We had to move out by the end of June! I went to the Lord myself and asked, "If we're not to look for a house, what should we be doing in the meantime?" The only thing I heard was, "Adore Me."

Let me tell you, I did not obey Jesus because I was full of confidence. I wish I could look back and say I had absolutely no doubt at all things were going to pan out beautifully. However, that wasn't the case. I was sick with worry. Yet the best option to take was to give God a chance and do what He told us to do. Every evening, we gathered as a family and had communion with Hawaiian bread and cranberry juice. As poignant as that sounds on paper, if you were there, you would not have felt like we were getting anything holy accomplished. Sometimes the juice would spill. Sometimes the dog would steal a piece of bread. The kids were distracted. The parents were stressed. Yet we would go around saying what we most loved about our Jesus.

- "He's nice to us!"
- "He makes sure we have food every day!"
- "He forgave us our sins."
- "He is there for us when we're sad!"

Sometimes I'd clean up after our nightly communion wondering if we were being utterly foolish. I'm sure the servants in the preparation room at the wedding experienced a similar discomfort. Instead of telling them where to find some wine or what to substitute for the wine, Jesus gave them instructions that seemed entirely off topic. He told them to get the six stone water jars that were for Jewish purification and fill them up with water (that's a lot of water!)—each jar carried twenty to thirty gallons. How in the world was all this water going to fix the problem of no wine?

Doing as Jesus tells us to do will not always make sense. It will not always satiate our carnal need to control the situation we are in. Sometimes, God's directions will make absolute sense, but not always. Why did Noah have to build an ark on dry land? Why did the Israelite army have to quietly march around the walls of Jericho? Why did Elijah have people pour water onto the altar that he needed to see lit on fire? God's power is in His words. The grace to steward His power is found in adhering to His instructions, as mysterious and confounding as they may be at times.

Eventually, my husband and I found ourselves at an open house on June 7, 2020. After searching for a week, we had been turned away by every real estate agent in the area, mainly because, by this point, we had gone six months without income. We drove onto a bright, open property at 11 A.M. The house was everything we needed to raise four growing children, two dogs, and a church. We asked why all the windows of the house were open. To our utter amazement, the real estate agent casually explained that the house was being aired out because they just finished renovations before—get this—the *end of May.* After the walkthrough of the house, we sheepishly looked at the agent and gave him the rundown of reality. It started with, "So, we're church planters, and we don't have a guaranteed income." He looked at us carefully as we gave him the full picture of what we were dealing with. Then he said, "You know, for some reason, you guys look like good people." We signed the contract and got the keys by 1 P.M. Not only that, but this home also ended up being in the exact town that we launched Mosaic Covenant Church. We built our launch team there. We ministered to neighbors there. We held prayer meetings and praise team practices there. How? We just did whatever Jesus told us to do.

I love that the first people to experience Jesus's first sign were the servants. Can you imagine the shock and awe they must have felt as the water they drew was wine by the time it reached the headwaiter? What an honor it must have been to be a servant in the preparation room at that wedding in Cana! An anonymous servant carrying out Jesus's instructions walks in more spiritual power than a rich and famous person with all the resources in the world.

ALL FOR HIS GLORY

Let's make sure not to mistake the moment. This isn't about how Jesus gives gold stars to the obedient. It's also not a random act of kindness that Jesus arbitrarily chooses to hand out. The purpose of God's miracles isn't to convince us to behave or make our lives easier to manage. God's power is not solely for our inspiration or our self-betterment. The very essence of God's power is redemptive, and every miracle it produces points to Jesus. We can see this by the impact of the miracle at the wedding.

> He revealed his glory, and his disciples believed in him.*

Every God-given miracle will glorify and point to Jesus. It was neither to build momentum, nor to garner the attention of a million subscribers. There was no political agenda or financial gain. It was just for a few people to recognize Christ.

Why wait for the next revival service to be held at your church to see people come to Christ? Why tether the movement of the Holy Spirit to a date on a calendar or a name on a flyer? There doesn't need to be a grand, curated event to give your loved ones a chance to befriend Jesus. Can God work mightily in these things? Absolutely. But I want to encourage you to open your mind to the ways God can move. Every ordinary moment has holy potential to bring to faith your circle of friends, that fellow regular at the gym, or even the barista at your favorite café.

Even your problems are an opportunity for someone to believe. This great miracle in Cana began with a problem. There was an unexpected and incredibly inconvenient need. A miscalculation of beverages at a party was what started it all. It was a disruption no one asked for, and yet it's a moment that's been

* John 2:11.

blessing people for centuries. How acclimated are we to simply complain over inconveniences? When our plans do not go smoothly, we often call it spiritual warfare rather than a heavenly opportunity to invite Jesus in. When we end a day of unexpected conflict, do we pray that it will get easier or do we pray that Jesus will glorify Himself through it?

PUT IT INTO PRACTICE

1. What overlooked or seemingly irrelevant area in your life can you offer to Jesus to use for His glory?
2. What is Jesus telling you to do in this season?
3. Is there a need that you haven't invited Him into?
4. Has Jesus done a miracle in your life that you haven't shared about with others? With whom can you share it?

9

FEED THE THOUSANDS

The story of Jesus feeding the thousands is one of the most iconic miracles in the Bible, so much so that even those who have never set foot in a church have likely heard about it. It's a real-life account of one of God's many works. A crowd of thousands, many of whom were sick and disabled, grew weak under the heat of the sun and the lack of replenishment. A laughably insufficient offering of five loaves and two fish was placed in front of Jesus. The overwhelmed disciples, pressured for solutions, said it was not enough. Jesus said otherwise, and that meager offering was endlessly broken apart to feed the desperate masses, five thousand men and even more women and children. Believe it or not, God is still doing miracles like this all around the world. We are just so accustomed to serving by our own calculated capacity and rationed strength that we have not positioned ourselves to witness God's supernatural replenishment.

A meal of chili and rice for a family of four still multiplies to satisfy a hundred orphans in Mozambique. Meager rations of emergency food at a pantry in Kentucky still distribute to five times more families than was expected. A church in the Philippines opens their kitchens to feed a hundred people a week, only to be met with twice that many one day and witness every mouth abundantly fed. When you listen for the testimonies of believers (and not just your go-to teachers on YouTube), you get a pulse on what Jesus is doing around the world. These moments may not be written about in your favorite *New York Times* bestselling book or talked about in your go-to podcast, but they come from the mouths of everyday Christians across the globe who are about the Father's work. Upon hearing and reading about these stories myself, I have noticed a through line in all of them: *Multiplication miracles are compelled by the compassion to serve beyond our available means.* All these miracles begin with lack.

THE BURDEN AND BLESSING OF LACK

"God knows the pressure you feel about your finances," said a praying woman I just met. She was a friend of a friend, and that was the extent of our connection. All I knew of her was that she was an entrepreneur whose main calling from God was to pray for people and that my friend wanted me to meet her. She sat across from me at a café, and she kindly looked into my eyes and said those words. I knew instantly that it was the Holy Spirit giving her prophetic knowledge because otherwise she could not know that I was daily riddled with worries about making a living as a young church pastor. When I chose vocational church ministry, it was because I wanted to dedicate my entire life to preaching the gospel and ushering souls toward the transformative power of the Holy Spirit. I wasn't counting the cost . . . at first.

At that time in my life, I was counting every nickel and dime. I rationed my groceries. I would stay home to avoid having to spend more on gas. At one point, the front headlights of my car were on their last leg, and I did not have the funds to change them out. I remember driving down I-5 late at night, having my windows down to help me see, the pitch-black ocean alongside me, with one dead headlight and the other slowly dimming, desperately praying that Jesus would sustain that last light until my next paycheck (which He did, by the way). This "friend of a friend" could not have known any of this, and yet the way she was looking at me made me feel like she understood. She didn't offer me any solutions, only encouragement that I need not worry and just had to trust God (which, I thought, was easy to say coming from someone who owned multiple businesses). However, after leaving that meeting, the Holy Spirit instructed me with this: *Everything you have is from Me. Give when I tell you to give, and you will experience no lack.*

Let's just say, He told me to give quite often from then on. Whether it was to buy a struggling student a new shirt for Sunday services or to give everything in my wallet to someone on the street, I was tempted to count the cost. Yet as I stopped hoarding my resources as my own, supernatural provision started to come in. A married couple that I'd never met at church reached out to me and testified that the Lord spoke to them and instructed them to support me with a certain amount each month for a time. Also, unexpected side gigs and tutoring jobs came my way. In time, I realized I was free to preach the gospel and minister to my students because the matter of my survival was up to God, not me. My little monthly paycheck that just barely covered rent eventually became a full-fledged living that supported school, ministry, and a blessed life in Southern California. What was not enough became more than enough.

Lack is emotionally exhausting, especially if endured for a long time. We don't have to be working in ministry to know this tension, and it doesn't have to be a matter of money. It can be the felt absence of energy, time, peace, purpose, significance, connection, freedom—essentially anything that causes us to live with a *need for more.* It's usually that very sense of insufficiency that keeps us discounting ourselves from becoming vessels for God's supernatural compassion. For some, lack isn't just an inconvenience. It can feel like a threat too. Not enough influence can feel like a threat to our identity. Not enough time can feel like a threat to our happiness. We hoard to combat this threat, but if we are preoccupied with hoarding for ourselves, we will never know the power of being Christ's hands and feet. The hoarding mindset may sound like this:

- "I'll help out when life slows down for me."
- "I know my co-worker is struggling, but I am too."
- "I can only pray for myself because I have so many needs."
- "I don't have time to help others because I'm too busy keeping up."
- "I'll donate more when I have enough saved up."

Now, Friend, this does not mean you ignore your limitations or force yourself to disregard them. The religiously legalistic spin to all of this would be to dishonor your basic needs to be useful to God. Jesus does not call us to ignore our reality. Jesus encouraged His disciples to go away with Him to secluded areas to rest when they were running low on physical and emotional fuel.* Ultimately though, our lack should not determine our obedience to Christ. If Jesus tells us to help, serve, or give when there's not enough, we help, serve, or give anyway. It is only then that lack goes from being a burden to a blessing.

While in front of a hungry crowd, the disciples said what any reasonable person would say: "Send the crowds away."† In other words, "Get rid of this burden!" Do you ever pray a similar prayer? Maybe it sounds like, "Jesus, please make my debt go away." "Please make this person who drains me go away." "Make this problem disappear." The disciples were in hoarding mode. They wanted to hoard whatever food, money, and energy they had left. In this moment, they forgot that they were servants of God with access to the power of the Holy Spirit. Instead, they resorted to being humans who wanted fewer problems. We can forget as well, believing only for our own survival instead of for other people's blessings.

Instead of waving a magic wand and allowing the disciples to bypass the need for faith, Jesus said, "They don't need to go away. . . . You give them something to eat."‡ When Jesus does not remove the lack, it is because the lack is not a burden that will destroy us. Instead, it is the birthplace of faith and the starting point of blessing. Jesus was raising the disciples to be servants, just as He is a servant. So, when the disciples touted their inability to serve because of lack, Jesus disagreed. In the

* Mark 6:31.

† Matthew 14:15.

‡ Matthew 14:16.

same way, you can still evangelize even if you're a new believer with seemingly insufficient knowledge of the Bible. You can still show up for your neighbor even if your house isn't clean and your freezer has only microwavable pizza. You can still minister in your workplace with your one-minute prayers in the elevator and five-minute intercession during breaks. Don't let your lack lie to you and tell you that you are useless for the kingdom of God. The Holy Spirit within you is the Great Multiplier. He is so creative that He formed the whole earth out of a meaningless void. He knows what to do with what you have.

THE CARE OF JESUS

One of my children once told me that he didn't ask me for a toy because, "I assumed you would say no." It's how he said it that caught my attention. It wasn't an expensive game, so it wasn't a matter of cost. After sitting him down and talking it out, I realized that he figured I cared only about his faith and grades and not about his fun. How he approached me was determined by what he thought was important to *me,* and to spare himself the disappointment, he didn't bother asking about the other things that mattered to him. I explained to him that I care about those things because I care about all of him, not just the church and school parts. *He* is what matters to me, not just his behaviors. It was a sweet interchange, one that was revelatory for me as well.

We do the same thing as children of God! We tend to hold back on praying and believing because of similar reasons, don't we? We think, *Maybe Jesus doesn't care about my need for a new car or an extra nap. He may care about the salvation of my uncle's soul, but maybe it's not important enough to ask Him about my cousin's college tuition.*

You need to know how much Jesus cares about all of who you are, or else you will allow your faith to be fragmented, allowing only *parts of you* to be yielded to the Holy Spirit's power. If you do not understand the scope of God's compassion, you will pray only about your spiritual needs while striving to manage your physical, mental, and emotional needs on your own. Understanding God's care for you gives you permission to fully activate your faith. It releases you to pray not only for a pure heart but also for that annoying pain in your lower back that your nightly stretches and Advil can't seem to fix. If you ever doubt that God cares about the full range of your humanity, just look at how Jesus responded to others even in His own moment of pain.

After John the Baptist died, the last thing Jesus needed was people making more demands. When He heard about His cousin's death, He purposely withdrew to be alone to pray. He needed it. He is God, but He experienced the full range of emotion as any human would. The grief drove Him into solitude, and He needed to refuel in the presence of His Father. Kind of like when a mother of little children hides in the pantry for a minute to breathe, or when we sit in the car for a time to gather ourselves before the next thing. Yet what interrupted Jesus's time to refill Himself was a multitude in pursuit of His time and attention. He could have turned them away. He could have hidden. These were not necessarily people who were looking for Jesus to believe and be saved. They wanted their physical needs met. They wanted pain to go away. And Jesus cared about that, deeply.

One of the clearest signs of the Holy Spirit in you is a supernatural tenderness toward those who are suffering. *God's power makes love visible.* Jesus's compassion wasn't charitable pity. It was a divine force that compelled Him to serve beyond His capacity.

I once led a prayer meeting in a fellow church member's home. About thirty people sat in the living room to pray for our church community. Yet we felt led to spend the last few minutes of prayer contending for the foster children of our region, as well as the foster care system. I felt the Holy Spirit gently sweep through the room, and soon, sniffles were heard. When I looked around, many were wiping tears. I'd never seen this side of this group before. I didn't know they cared that much! It was the anointing of the Holy Spirit that empowered us with mercy. It was as if we were feeling what the Father felt about the foster children in New Jersey.

The Holy Spirit's power reveals the beating heart of our heavenly Father. He is the Father that counts our hairs,* keeps track of our sorrows,† and cares about our anxieties.‡ Friend, we must be convinced that Jesus cares about the whole of who we are as humans. His heart breaks for the children in unstable living conditions, and the sorrow of people starving in war-torn regions of the world floods His heart. At the same time, He cares about you having enough sleep. He cares about your spouse's alcohol addiction. He cares that you need more space in your home. Jesus cared about the crowd's ailments, and He also cared that they received something to eat. Compassion gave birth to the miracle.

I once knew of a young man who desired to grow in the gift of healing. In our circle, we knew of several people who would regularly pray for those with sickness and disabilities and see

* Luke 12:6–7.

† Psalm 56:8.

‡ 1 Peter 5:7.

visible results after the prayer. Praise Jesus! This young man longed for the ability to minister as they did. He would regularly go around trying to pray for anyone who may need physical healing, even a bit invasively at times. He became increasingly discouraged by the lack of results. After watching him grow in frustration, a mutual brother in Christ challenged him with this thought: "Do you care about those with sickness and disabilities?" His point made this young man pause to reflect. He coveted the power to heal, but he did not have compassion for those who needed healing. The disciples had to learn this too. They did not realize that Jesus wasn't there merely to perform healings. He was there to care for the crowd. Their lack of compassion nearly caused them to reject the opportunity for one of the most memorable miracles in history. If we live to perform, produce, or please, we give when it's good enough. Christlike compassion compels us to give what little we have, whether it is good enough or not.

BLESS THE LORD

What do you usually do with lack? What's your go-to response to insufficiency? The first five years of church planting involved constantly glancing at my checking account. It felt like there was never enough. We needed more funding, more volunteers, more space to meet—it was endless. When I wasn't activating my faith, I defaulted to complaining, calculating, and hoarding. Sometimes, if I was deeply entrenched in discouragement, I felt as though God was holding back on us. I've been humbled time and time again by the example that Jesus set in the face of lack. What did He do while holding this short supply of food in front of the hungry crowd? He blessed the Lord.

When Jesus took the five loaves and two fish, He looked up to the heavens and blessed them. What He likely did was pray a prayer of thanks as any head of the family typically would before a meal. An example of this traditional prayer was as follows:

> Blessed art thou, O Lord our God, King of the universe, who bringest forth bread from the earth.*

Jesus blessed the Provider of the five loaves and two fish. How often do we go to God wanting more, more, and more? How much of our prayer life is preoccupied with asking Jesus to fix and provide? Here, Jesus was faced with a massive conflict. Thousands of hungry souls and stomachs. Only five loaves and two fish. Calling it lack would fail to capture the gravity of the situation. This was a crisis. As a planner myself, I can only imagine how the disciples felt, counting the money required to feed them, calculating the time it would take to find the food and the manpower involved in bringing the food back. Yet all Jesus did was praise the Lord. He blessed Him with thanks.

Whenever God blesses us, we're endowed with grace and favor. Whenever someone was blessed by God throughout Bible history, His presence with them would empower them to be fruitful in some way. Yet when we bless God, we can't make Him stronger or happier than He already is. We gain everything when God blesses us. What He gets when we bless Him is our faith. The greatest act of faith in dire times is to bless the Lord and praise Him with all our heart! Before the breakthrough.

* Donald A. Hagner, *Matthew 14–28,* vol. 33B, Word Biblical Commentary (Word, 1995), 418.

Before the victory. Before the miracle. Praise Him! This, too, is a way to steward the Holy Spirit's power in us. It's not a time to complain for more or stockpile what we need. Mind you, there is value in hard work and good planning. God works through this as well. Jesus simply postured Himself to be ready for what God planned on doing with the five loaves and two fish.

Ultimately, it is the anointing of the Holy Spirit that turns insufficiency into abundance. There is no power in our complaining and controlling. Our part to play is our faith. How can we act in faith in the face of lack? Bless Him. Magnify Jesus with your praises despite your desperate circumstances. Bless Him for the thirty-five dollars left in your savings. Bless Him for the little energy you have to move around today. Bless Him for the one friend who stuck around. Bless Him for the job you've been trying to get promoted from. Bless the Lord, because lack should not stop you from glorifying Jesus!

ABUNDANCE AND AUTHORITY

There was a reason for the twelve baskets full of leftovers. Jesus wanted the disciples to understand something. He was trying to awaken them to His complete and unrivaled authority and consequently the authority He was going to delegate to them through the anointing of the Holy Spirit. Living by God's authority and not our own self-made power is a paradigm shift that every Christian must make. We live in a world that teaches us that we make things happen by seizing, protecting, and performing. We're told to climb the ladder, outshine the competition, and take control. Jesus taught the disciples a different way: "Look at all these leftovers. Look at this abundance." It wasn't just one basket but twelve—like the twelve tribes of

Israel—to remind us that God's provision is sufficient for *all* His people. And it came by Christ's authority.

There was a time when lack didn't exist, and it was when humankind honored the reign of God and exercised their own delegated authority in perfect harmony with Him. In the Garden of Eden, abundance was a way of life. Because God is good, His dominion brings life, growth, and fruitfulness. It was His presence that made all things grow! The reality in the garden did not reflect being behind on rent, wrestling through red tape to get food stamps, or living paycheck to paycheck. It was when Adam and Eve stopped trusting in God's rulership, thereby forfeiting their spiritual authority to the enemy, that they experienced lack and the sting of the curse. Genesis 3:17–19 describes it:

> The ground is cursed because of you.
> You will eat from it by means of painful labor
> all the days of your life.
> It will produce thorns and thistles for you,
> and you will eat the plants of the field.
> You will eat bread by the sweat of your brow
> until you return to the ground.

Working to the bone only to be the guarantors of our own survival was never our destiny as God's children. The Creator did not design us to pointlessly run on a hamster wheel of self-preservation until the end of our days. We were created to rule and reign as His children, commissioned as ambassadors of His presence on this earth. To live for our survival was the fruit of the curse but never what we were designed for. Our humble King came to reinstate what Adam and Eve forfeited in the garden. God has delegated His power back to us, in the name of Jesus, giving us authority to bring life wherever we go.

Every piece of leftover bread and fish the disciples collected was a reminder to trust in Christ's authority. They had enough to fill twelve baskets, one for each disciple. If God cared enough to leave them with leftover baskets full of provision, then surely they were free to set aside self-preservation while living to love generously. They had to trust this in order to steward the anointing of the Holy Spirit. This is not to say that if you place your faith in Christ He will fulfill all your earthly dreams for vacations, cars, and houses. Rather, faith in Christ will not leave you lacking, and you are free to follow Him, trusting that no lack can stand in the way of His power.

PUT IT INTO PRACTICE

1. Whom do you lack compassion for? Ask the Holy Spirit to create a Christlike compassion in you.
2. How can you serve others with what's in your hands, even if it may not be perfect or enough?
3. What lack can you bless the Lord for today?

10

WALK ON WATER

I knew someone who once tried to walk on water, just to test it out. He was clad in a wetsuit and rose-colored optimism when he stepped onto the pool water . . . and immediately sank right in. Guffaws and knee-slapping laughter erupted post-splash. The reason why we weren't tinged with disappointment was because we knew that Jesus did not walk on water just to encourage believers to casually defy the laws of physics for entertainment.

While on earth, Jesus always operated beyond the realm of human possibility, and we tend to shrug it off with, "Well, of course. He's God." But let's pause there and not forget that He also lived among us as fully man, bound by the same limitations that you and I have. His life was not the exception but, rather, the example by which we are to live today. Jesus lived perfectly in sync with His Father, and everything He did was the fruit of this intimate alignment—including walking on water.

We can know one thing after reading this account in the Gospels: Faith isn't just about witnessing God do the miraculous; it's also about stepping into it with Him. There was something raw and terrifying about this scene: a boat battered by waves and the dilapidated disciples, weary and wet from the winds that bullied them through the night. If you've ever tried doing anything through the night, you know just how depleted the disciples must have been. And then bone-chilling screams as the men try fixing their eyes on who—or what—is walking toward them. Could it be a ghost? Wait, was that *Jesus* walking toward them?

Jesus walking on water is proof that the anointed life is not neat and tidy. We're not here to achieve a cookie-cutter sort of Christianity, the kind that behaves well but doesn't burn with Holy Spirit power. It's not without suffering. It's not without some hazy, confusing moments. We're talking about walking straight into howling winds and bullying waves with God-given spiritual authority. Those who walk on water trust God to tell them what really is possible. Like Christ, they do not succumb to chaos and turmoil because they have the spiritual authority to walk over it.

KEEP HIDING IN PRAYER

Everything Jesus did overflowed from a hidden place of prayer. Some call it a "secret place," which is defined not solely by its absence of people but, rather, by its exclusivity to God. Jesus hid to unveil the inner room of His heart to His Father. It's where secrets were mutually exchanged. The happenings of this secret place were not for show. It was the watering hole that Christ depended on. Did Jesus have one designated place to hide with His Father? No, He simply hid where and when He could, because the secret place is not a physical location but, rather, a posture of prayer. The kind where His presence is prioritized above everyone else's presence. It's guarded because it's a sacred interaction, and wherever it takes place is holy ground.

As public as He was throughout his three-year ministry, Jesus always retreated to be alone with His Father in heaven. What marked this hiddenness was not that He hid from people. Instead, He consistently hid *in* the presence of God by prayer.* If you are struggling to imagine what this is like, let's refer to King David's words in Psalm 32:6–7:

> Let everyone who is faithful pray to you immediately.
> When great floodwaters come,
> they will not reach him.
> You are my hiding place;
> you protect me from trouble.
> You surround me with joyful shouts of deliverance. *Selah*

The presence of God is a hiding place. When you shift your focus toward Him and start addressing Jesus, you are running into a spiritual fortress, unseen by the naked eye but a real, supernatural refuge. Of course, God uses people, places, and things to protect you, but His presence itself is also a haven. This was what kept King David safe amid the tumult that incessantly hounded him. He praised and prayed through failure, betrayal, war, and loss. As long as he hid in God's presence,

* Luke 5:16.

King David had armor and weapons that not even the shrewdest of enemies was able to see.

This is why Jesus would get away to pray. He was giving His Father private access to His attention. Everything He did was the result of this intentionally tended communion. He chose His disciples after He hid to pray. He decided where to minister after He hid to pray. He also fed the thousands and walked on water after He'd been in prayer.

Jesus was consistent and persistent about His private moments with His Father. If you recall, before He fed the thousands, Jesus withdrew by a boat to a remote place to be alone in prayer. Yet the crowds—and all the clamoring needs that came with them—found Him. Distractions will always find you! Nevertheless, what's beautiful is that Jesus let the needy crowd interrupt Him because His habit of praying in the secret place was not a religious rule that lorded over Him. Still, after He was done serving the crowds, He sent the disciples ahead of Him on a boat and dismissed the crowd of thousands so He could go back to His original intent, which was to be alone in prayer. He was persistent. Life happens, as it did for Jesus. Intentionally finding alone time is a simple choice, but it's also a costly one. Can you imagine how much work it must have taken for Jesus to be alone? To coordinate with His disciples and shout directions for a needy crowd to leave Him was no light feat. He may have had to escape the crowd even after He dismissed them. Even so, it did not deter Him from going right back into that secret place.

As a pastor, I find myself interacting with many Christians who feel downtrodden with guilt about not finding enough time to pray. It could be a mom of young children. An on-call medical specialist. Flight attendants with unpredictable schedules. We can plan all we want, and yet the demands of life will find us. If that is you, then I encourage you to be like Jesus! Do what you must and go right back into the secret place. Self-condemnation and religious pressure will not produce intimacy with the Holy Spirit. Go back and choose prayer again. After all, that's what Jesus did.

Being alone with God has a cost, and only those who know how much they need the Holy Spirit's power are willing to pay it. Going home an hour earlier than your friends do during a night out to sit with Jesus has a cost. Getting on your knees for five minutes before your baby wakes up has a cost. Forfeiting the hours of self-soothing television watching and phone scrolling has a cost. It's a disruption. It takes effort. Even those who work in churches and ministry offices have difficulty paying this cost. It also costs to be alone and to go to such a deep place with the Holy Spirit that no one fully understands. We will willingly pay the cost only when we realize this truth: The cost of not praying is higher than the cost of prayer because kingdom works require God's power.

Just like Jesus, an anointed Christian is persistently hiding in the presence of God. Any believer can experience a moment of wonder with Jesus, whether it's a revelatory dream, healing, or something else. However, to continuously walk in the power of the Holy Spirit requires a consistent choice to retreat into prayer. If you've never done this before or struggle to begin, a great starting point is to choose whatever is most consistent in your day. Could it be your drive to work? Your time to sit down for emails? Your evening showers? Choose those pockets of opportunity to intentionally realign yourself with Jesus. Don't worry about what you should be experiencing or feeling as you make this choice. Even being met with silence doesn't make your choice a failure. The Bible never said that Jesus came away from His secret-place prayer time abounding with elated tears and new liturgy from heaven. All we know for sure is that He made the choice to hide in prayer often, and so should we. Dismiss the world and go hide, Friend.

HAVE COURAGE

The anointing gives us spiritual authority, but *courage activates that authority.* Without courage, spiritual authority lies dormant within us. It's normal to be afraid, but we are not accessing what we are carrying when we remain in fear's grip. When the winds blow, some may resort to complaining and blaming. When the waves threaten us, it's easier to wallow in anxiety. It does not take any spiritual authority to do these things. This is why, when God calls us to do the difficult or even impossible, He commands us to be courageous first.

> As the Israelites were preparing to take on the promised land, God told them to "be strong and courageous."*
>
> As Joshua took on the enormous task of leading Israel, God told him to "be strong and courageous."†
>
> As David was readying his son Solomon to build the temple, he said by the Spirit of the Lord, "be strong and courageous."‡

* Deuteronomy 31:6.
† Joshua 1:6–7.
‡ 1 Chronicles 22:13.

To the disciples as Jesus was preparing them for His crucifixion, He said, "Be courageous!"*

So, how can we muster up courage? Do we wait for a swell of confidence to rush in, or do we fake it until we make it? When Jesus looked on the frantic faces of His cold and clinging disciples in the boat, He said, "Have courage! It is I. Don't be afraid."† This wasn't a "pull yourself up by the bootstraps" sort of command. A courageous Christian is not someone who manages to maintain a stiff upper lip through trials.

I'm going to get a little detailed here, but bear with me. When Jesus instructs us to be courageous, He is not telling us to ignore the winds and waves. This is not an invitation to some sort of sanctioned denial. After the command for courage, Jesus said, "It is I," which in Greek is *egō eimi.* Whenever Jesus said any rendition of *egō eimi* in the Gospels, it was a divine revelation. It's much like when God said to Moses, "I AM WHO I AM."‡ Amid the chaos, Jesus revealed Himself to His disciples because this fresh revelation was the antidote to their fear.

Can we really know who God is unless we see Him amid our troubles? We don't really know a person until we've seen them through both sunshine and storms. I've had the honor of serving alongside many people over the years in church ministry. At the start of the co-laboring journey, all I see are their strengths and gifts, especially when things are new and exciting. However, it's how they walk through rejection, disappointment, and failure that reveals the gold inside them. When I see resilience, hope, and humility shine through during hard times, I see them

* John 16:33.

† Matthew 14:27.

‡ Exodus 3:14.

in a whole new light. It causes me to admire them in a new way, and it creates deeper confidence in me to work alongside them. In a similar vein, as the disciples recognized Jesus atop the very waves they were terrified of, they got to know Him in a way they never had before. Not only that, but they also realized that they were never alone in their troubles after all.

The revelation of God's presence isn't just knowing that He's real. It's a fresh spiritual awareness of who He is and what He's capable of, as well as His nearness to us. Recognizing God's presence does not eradicate the chill of fear, but it does produce courage. Everything changes when we realize who's with us! When my family and I moved into a new neighborhood, we were a bit wary of our new surroundings. It was a typical suburban town, but we moved in during a time when there was news of break-ins and car thefts across town. It was a bigger house, and the master bedroom felt farther away from our children's rooms than we were initially comfortable with. So, what did we do? We got a German shepherd puppy. Once our little Lady grew up to a full-fledged watchdog, there was newfound peace in the home. Every noise wasn't a threat. Our children were free to wander about the property, with Lady following them around, of course. It's not that we became braver or stronger by any means; we just knew that Lady was always with us, and we knew what she was capable of.

Maybe you could use a reminder of who you're with today. Of course, your problems may feel insurmountable. You don't need to deny the presence of conflict. No need to pretend that the overhanging debt, toxic work conditions, or your past choices are not a problem. *But do you know who you're with?* God laid the foundations of the earth with His very words. He moved waters to create paths. He kept the sun still for a day so that battles could be won. He allowed a boy to slay a giant. He kept three men from burning in fire. He used pagan kings for His glory. He has loved the dead to life. His mercy has sustained His church through persecution, heresy, hypocrisy, division, corruption, cultural compromise, political manipulation, and spiritual apathy. Need I say more? Nothing has stopped Him from loving you and remaining with you. Have courage. It is Jesus, and He's with you.

I've walked through several terrifying seasons, but one season that stands out is when I had just given birth to my third child. Being that she arrived a month early, we were not expecting her to be born on the very day we were moving into a new house. She arrived at 4 A.M., and the moving truck was scheduled to come at 7 A.M. Not only that, but my newborn girl was rushed to the NICU five minutes after birth. It was a maelstrom of madness, to say the least, but we got through it. It wasn't until a few weeks later that the real storm hit. A letter came in the mail—it was the bill from the hospital. The color left my husband's face as he stood in the kitchen in disbelief. Along with the moving, the NICU visits, and becoming a family of five a month earlier than expected, my husband and I were also both in a job transition that affected some due processes with our health insurance. It was an administrative hiccup, but in short, my daughter's time in the intensive care unit was not covered by insurance, with the consequences being a bill that was comparable to a down payment on a house.

For the next few hours, my husband and I exchanged very few words out of sheer disbelief. My mind desperately tried to hold on to the narrative of hope and faith, but fear kept hijacking the narrative and rewriting it with panic. We agreed, when the baby was napping, to spend the next hour in our separate corners of the house to seek the Lord's counsel. For the first few minutes, I tried to pray, to no avail. I was drowning in worry. So I began to sing instead—whatever it took to interrupt my body's survival instincts with an acknowledgment of His presence. By the end of the hour, the only words I had heard from the Lord were, "Don't be afraid. Take it step by step. I will give Dave wisdom." Confused, I left my prayer corner to tell my husband, who was also coming out of his own prayer corner, what I'd heard. He nodded like he fully understood what I was saying. From there, we began a yearlong journey of tackling this bill, step by step. Some of the payments were covered by what we allotted from our paychecks. Other payments were provided for, whether it was a bonus here or a gift from a generous giver there. After a year, there was one payment left. My husband was on the phone with the same hospital financial counselor that he'd been working with all year, and to his bewilderment, this counselor looked at our outstanding bill of a few thousand dollars and said, "Don't worry about this one. It will be covered." I even asked my ob-gyn if this was something that happened regularly, and he said he'd never heard of such a thing. Look at God!

We didn't know it then, but that unexpected hospital bill was God's invitation for us to walk on water with Him. The choice to have courage was our yes to that invitation. We needed to face the winds and waves and make that first call to the hospital's billing office, despite our trepidation. Courage dared us to remain obedient even when fear was intimidatingly loud. Not only did my husband and I pay off this hospital bill to completion, but by the end of that year, we were in the best financial standing we've ever been in in our marriage! We could not have done it on our own. What started off as an emergency became a journey of God doing what only He can do.

AUTHORITY OVER WINDS AND WAVES

When I was a mother to young children, preaching became the whole family's business because every sermon required multiple sets of eyes and hands looking after my children. Every once in a while, as I preached, I'd see one or two of my kids press their faces on the glass doors at the sanctuary entrance. They'd watch me. They'd watch the people sitting and listening. They'd listen to the sound of my voice. Eventually, they obtained a subtle understanding that Mommy was in charge when she was holding the microphone. In turn, one of my children assumed that because I had authority, he had it too. Even with multiple people keeping an eye on him, he would still manage to occasionally burst through the sanctuary doors and march down the aisle toward the pulpit. Without a care of who was watching or what they were thinking, he'd stand next to my legs or lift his three-year-old hands to be held. This toddler with no inherent strength or power had more boldness than the average adult by assuming the following: *I can do this because my mom is in charge.*

Although he later learned that there was a time and place for these things, his logic at that time wasn't entirely wrong when attributed to the spiritual sense. In fact, Peter shared a similar line of reasoning. He saw his Rabbi walking on the very thing he was afraid of. This was his Messiah who had also commissioned him with spiritual authority not long before.* He

* Matthew 10.

thought that maybe he, too, could walk on water because Jesus was in charge. Although Peter was just flesh and bones, spiritual authority is God's delegated power to fulfill His purpose on earth. And that changes everything.

I started working at the church when I was nineteen, and I did it with fear and trembling. I'll be the first to admit I love the comfortable and peaceful life. I would avoid trouble if I could, and the way I led and interacted with people reflected that. Although I tried my best to serve the church, I also did my best to please and pacify people. I did not realize that by doing so, I was stifling my God-given spiritual authority. I wasn't using the anointing God gave me. I was the disciple who avoided the winds and waves instead of itching for the invitation to walk over them. Although I knew that some of the students did not know Jesus and had yet to be saved, I had to navigate the pressures from parents who wanted me only to make sure that their kids were well behaved and committed to school. So, in my first three years of serving and leading in the church, I avoided many conflicts but witnessed very few souls saved, bodies healed, and hearts delivered from darkness.

We cannot avoid the tempests of life if we want to truly experience the power of God. It's like a mountain climber avoiding heights while yearning to conquer the summit. Or a singer avoiding performing while dreaming to be the next Grammy-awarded artist. The disciples who remained in the boat will never be able to share what it was like to feel the cold water under their feet, propping them up instead of swallowing them whole. Friend, are you living with avoidance or authority?

Now, there *is* a line between faithfully stewarding your God-given spiritual authority and being presumptuous about what you can do. Bravado is not spiritual authority. Bold gestures and loud actions do not move heaven. On the contrary, it's our union with Jesus that empowers us. Notice that Peter said, "Command me to come to you on the water."* His ability depended on Jesus's permission. Peter's authority was limited to Jesus's will because God determines how much power He delegates to us. How do we determine Christ's will? We will find it in His words—in Scripture and through prayer.

LOCK YOUR GAZE

It's one thing to start something, and it's another to sustain it. Just like it's one thing to get married and another to stay married. It's one thing to start a cleaner diet, and it's another to maintain that healthy lifestyle. It's one thing to step out of the boat because of an inspired moment with Jesus, and it's another to keep walking on that water toward Him. Peter did for a moment, but the moment his gaze broke away from Jesus, he forfeited the spiritual authority he was in.

What you gaze at will determine who or what you have faith in. I've had many seasons of struggling deeply with anxiety. Every morning, I would be stuck in bed with paranoid thoughts and a sense of impending doom. There was one change I made that drastically made a difference and gave me the impetus to press forward. I stopped starting the day on social media. At first, it had felt like a harmless way to wake up from slumber. But I did not realize that starting the day by gazing at lies, opinions, and tragic news was gravely affecting my faith. The Bible is full of examples, as well, of people allowing their focus to influence them:

* Matthew 14:28.

When Eve and Adam set their sight on the fruit of the tree of the knowledge of good and evil, they chose to trust the fruit over their Creator.*

When Lot looked out and saw the well-watered plain of the Jordan, he pitched his tent near Sodom, a place of sin.†

As Stephen was being persecuted and then killed by stoning, he looked up and saw the glory of God, and he fearlessly became the first martyr for Christ.‡

You go where your eyes go. Your daily diet of sight determines the shape of your faith, and it will influence the way you steward spiritual authority. Peter was indeed walking on water. He was doing exactly as Jesus was doing. Yet when his gaze toward Jesus broke and his attention shifted to the magnitude of the wind, he sank! No wonder the author of the book of Hebrews reminded us to keep our eyes fixed on Jesus, "the pioneer and perfector of our faith."§ As long as we lock our gaze on Christ, the winds and waves will not be our enemy.

Remember the yearlong sickness I told you about at the start of this book? I was sinking that year. As I lay in bed, my eyes were fixed on my symptoms. When I opened my phone, my eyes were fixed on what everyone else was doing with their seemingly healthy, happy lives. And if not that, then my eyes were fixed on the statistics that came with my diagnosis. Or, through the lens of social media, I'd fixate on all the tragic

* Genesis 3.

† Genesis 13:10.

‡ Acts 7:55–60.

§ Hebrews 12:2.

things that were happening around the world that year. I was so engulfed in hopelessness, it took six months to begin telling my friends about what was going on in my life. I'll never forget the look on one friend's face when I shared my situation with her. She said, "Faith! Why haven't you told me about this?" I sheepishly shrugged, to which she replied, "We're going to pray about this. Jesus still heals!" The thing is, I knew this—at least, in the back of my mind I did. But in this moment, her faith interrupted my trance from despair and defeat. She reminded me to shift my gaze on Jesus again, and a few months later, her faith-filled encouragement proved to be very true indeed.

Where is your gaze today, Friend? What are the winds and waves that may be discouraging you from walking in spiritual authority? Ultimately, there are two types of Christians in the church: those who safely tremble in boats, and those who walk on water while living lives that are made possible only by the Holy Spirit. Imagine if our churches were filled with Christians who were willing to get their feet wet!

PUT IT INTO PRACTICE

1. How can you regularly hide in prayer? What would that look like for you today?
2. What are the winds and waves that God is calling you to walk over with spiritual authority?
3. Where is your gaze today? What are you fixated on?

11

HEAL THE SICK AND CAST OUT DEMONS

I was at an evening church gathering in Nias, Indonesia. Culturally, they run their worship services a bit differently than we do in America, but the Holy Spirit's presence is the same. I couldn't help but smile at the pleasure of watching the exuberant dancing and singing. The room was no bigger than the size of a classroom, but it was teeming with those who were hungry and thirsty for the presence of God. I found out later that the lovely girls wearing white dresses and floral headpieces and holding tambourines were orphans that the local church leaders were raising. They danced in tandem through every song. Some smiled gleefully, and others had their eyes tightly closed in earnest.

A song came on that I'd never heard before, but the chorus went something like this:

Bekerjalah ya Roh Kudus
Bertahtalah lebih lagi

UrapanMu, lawatanMu
Kaulah yang kuperlu
Kau terutama di hidupku

I had no idea what these words meant, since I didn't speak Bahasa, but the Holy Spirit in me understood. I felt heaven's love deep within me. Instinctively, in this unfamiliar land among strangers (who eventually became family), I felt surreally at home. I wept over this precious and holy current of love washing over me. It was the Holy Spirit responding to the worship and blessing us with His presence. Later, I learned that the lyrics of this song were a personal invitation for the Holy Spirit to work and reign. It was both a longing and an exaltation of His presence.

After a wave of His love finished its swell in the room, the dancing girls in the front knelt to the ground. I didn't see any clear cues as to who started this shift, whether it was the girls or the worship team on stage. It almost felt like everyone was in sync because they were following the same God. The kneeling girls started crying out to Jesus in unison. They shook their tambourines and lifted their voices. "Yesus! Yesus! Yesus!" The worship team on stage began doing the same, tarrying before the Lord. Everyone remained in position as they lingered and pressed in. "Yesus! Yesus! Yesus!" When I looked around, I saw the rest of the room with their hands lifted doing the same. Calling out to Jesus, longing for the Holy Spirit to manifest Himself in greater measure. We continued this for an extended period of time.

Then, without anyone taking over the scene, there was a shift in the atmosphere. A weighty presence was felt, and the people began to react. A shriek was heard in the back of the room, and prayer team members immediately rushed over and started praying to cast out demons. Then healings began, which we knew of because of the eruption of cheers and applause. Some happened on their own, and some were initiated by prayer team members laying their hands on the place of ailment. This room we were in began to look like a completely different room than what we started with. It was as if the Holy Spirit had come in and announced that there was a new sheriff in town and that every affliction and evil had to go in Jesus's name.

A similar thing happened when Philip introduced Jesus to Samaria. Unclean spirits fled with shrieks, and the paralyzed began to walk. The presence of God is everywhere, but He's also *somewhere.* In Samaria, He wasn't just transcendent—He was immanent. And where His presence is acknowledged and welcomed, darkness and all its work are evicted. He manifests in places where He is wanted, where faith makes room, and where hunger invites Him. Those who host the Holy Spirit can bring this heavenly partnership wherever they go. Can Jesus do whatever He wants, wherever He wants on His own? Surely. But Sam Storms explained it well when he said, "God has *delegated* his authority to us. It is not God's plan to settle all our spiritual disputes apart from our involvement. He wants to utilize the authority he has invested in us."*

When you embraced the grace of Jesus Christ and began your new life as a child of God, He made a holy investment in you with the anointing of the Holy Spirit. This anointing marks you as His and gives you access to know Him intimately,

* Sam Storms, *Practicing the Power: Welcoming the Gifts of the Holy Spirit in Your Life* (Zondervan, 2017), 157, emphasis in original.

authentically, and passionately. It makes you a carrier of not only a message but also His presence. To disregard this reality is like living with a nuclear bomb in your living room and treating it like any old vase. The enemy is not afraid of your good reputation and extensive knowledge of church tradition. He's afraid of the anointing in you and the possibility that you will one day realize what it's for.

HEALED AND WHOLE

Have you ever looked around, whether it is your home, your neighborhood, maybe even your workplace, and felt the need for a new kind of order? Maybe it's corruption, violence, or death that makes it feel like evil is running the show. Why? Because of the interchange that happened during the fall of Adam and Eve, Satan has a say in what goes on in this world. The matter of illness and spiritual oppression is not God's doing. Children afflicted with cancer, lives destroyed by mental illness, and heart disease widowing a traumatized spouse were not God's will for us when He created us in paradise. Although our afflictions can be a by-product of our faithless choices or our self-serving habits that are in agreement with the enemy, the presence and possibility of illness, brokenness, and torment in this world are a result of Satan's order. When Jesus began His ministry, He preached that "the kingdom of God has come near."* Essentially, He was saying what I felt in Nias that one victorious evening. A new sheriff is in town, and with Him comes a new order. Jesus's mission on earth was not to distribute free tickets to heaven that will come into effect once we die.

* Mark 1:15.

Salvation is not just relevant for us "one day." It changes our reality *now* because He has come to remove us from the shackles of evil's dominion.

Humanity was created for divine wholeness of spirit, body, and soul. The devil came to steal, kill, and destroy our humanity, which is why we are faced with the world we live in today. Jesus came that we may "have life and have it in abundance."* (There's that word *abundance* again!) This is why Jesus spent a large part of His ministry healing and restoring people back into wholeness—spiritually, physically, and mentally. Two frequently used Greek words for "healing" in the New Testament are *sōzō* and *iaomai. Sōzō* is applied to physical healing, deliverance from evil spirits, and salvation.† *Iaomai* is also applied to physical healing, inner healing (healing from the heart's wounds), and spiritual restoration.‡ God's idea of healing is not just about fixing that bad leg. It is about complete freedom. He really meant it when He said He wants you to have life and have it in abundance!

This is also why I speak of healing and deliverance together in one conversation here. One is for the restoration of the body and mind and the other is freedom from spiritual bondage. Yet, sometimes, these two things can intersect. For example, healing may follow deliverance. It's common in Western belief to separate our spiritual health from our mental and physical health, but we often see them intertwined in Scripture. The mute boy with seizures had an unclean spirit in Mark 9. The disabled woman who was bent over for eighteen years was afflicted by a demonic spirit in Luke 13. However, this doesn't

* John 10:10.

† Matthew 1:21; Mark 10:52; Luke 8:36.

‡ Matthew 13:15; Luke 4:18; James 5:16.

mean that every fever is a demon. Sometimes it's just our transient, imperfect bodies going through what they do in this world that has yet to be fully redeemed and restored by Christ's return. Sometimes we break a leg because we're clumsy, not because the devil is after us! So let's not go demonizing every illness and affliction. The point is, no matter the cause of pain, Jesus cares for our restoration.

According to John Wimber, "Of the 3,774 verses in the four gospels, 484 relate specifically to healing of physical and mental illness and the resurrection of the dead. More impressive, of the 1,257 narrative verses in the gospels, 484 verses—38.5 percent!—are devoted to describing Jesus's healing miracles."* Needless to say, if you want to be a Christian who does the things that Jesus does, then you cannot discount healing. It's not for the "specially gifted." It is for the everyday Christian who walks in the anointing of the Holy Spirit. What's marvelously mysterious about the way Jesus healed while on earth was that He was not constrained by any one method or formula. Sometimes He spit on the ground and made mud. Sometimes He touched the sick. Sometimes He just said a word. Sometimes He gave an authoritative command. Sometimes He rebuked the evil spirit causing the ailment. Sometimes it happened when someone took the initiative to touch His cloak. Sometimes it happened in gradual stages. There is wisdom in strategy, but there is no power in the strategy itself. The power is solely in the anointing of the Holy Spirit, which you have by the grace and mercy of Christ.

* John Wimber with Kevin Springer, *Power Healing* (Hodder and Stoughton, 1987), 59.

THE SPIRITUAL WARFARE OF ANOINTED CHRISTIANS

We can't desire to grow in the anointing of the Holy Spirit without also being prepared for the spiritual warfare that comes with it. As we walk in the filling of the Holy Spirit, the anointing empowers us, but it also makes the invisible war around us visible. The anointing of the Holy Spirit in us is not a neutral force. It has a way of antagonizing evil spirits and drawing the spiritually hungry. I share this not to heighten any sort of paranoia but, rather, to help you grow in confidence and understanding.

For so long, I really thought I was unlucky, that bad things just kept happening to me for no apparent reason. Many times after being filled by the Holy Spirit, I felt like a magnet for bad things and bad people. Once, I was teaching a class on the Holy Spirit, and while I was teaching, I heard my husband's voice in the other room on the phone defending me against someone who chose that very day and hour to call him to vent and rain down curses on me (she chose the wrong person to vent to, I'll tell you that much). Another time, I was simply walking down the streets of Manhattan, in the Tribeca area, and a man with a cane started chasing me. I had to run all the way to Soho to evade him! Also, can I talk about all the random mysterious illnesses I've had throughout my life? From childhood until now, I've had seasons of doctor visits that required multiple blood panels that left many doctors confused as to how to diagnose me. I've even been transferred to Mayo Clinic because of a rare autoimmune disorder that required multiple specialists working together to come up with a diagnosis, including my bloodwork being sent to a one-of-a-kind lab in Utah. It was a condition that later completely disappeared when I chose to go on a mission trip that summer. After a while, I started to realize that this was no coincidence or a bad lot in life. This was warfare, and what I was carrying was provoking the enemy.

When Jesus taught in the synagogue, a man with a demon inside him cried out, "What do you have to do with us, Jesus of Nazareth? Have you come to destroy us?"* Here, Jesus was anointed and teaching with authority, and this provoked the enemy to disrupt the gathering with an outcry. Even as Jesus entered the region of Gerasenes, a man possessed by many demons ran toward Him and cried, "What do you have to do with me, Jesus, Son of the Most High God? I beg you before God, don't torment me!"† When Paul and Silas were simply on their way to prayer, a slave girl with a demon spirit of divination followed them around for days, yelling, "These men, who are proclaiming to you a way of salvation, are the servants of the Most High God."‡ What this girl carried vexed Paul to the point where he cast it out and was sent to prison for it because the owners were upset they could no longer use her to make money. In all these instances, the enemy was disruptive. He sought to interrupt the work of the Holy Spirit, and yet he was powerless against the authority of Christ.

Friend, the devil does exist and he would be quite satisfied if you lived the rest of your life content with being well-behaved and comfortable. The moment you start living a Spirit-filled life and stewarding His power is the moment you are a threat to the evil one. So, how can you stay prepared?

* Mark 1:23–24.

† Mark 5:1–7.

‡ Acts 16:16–18.

Be Sure of Who You Are

When Jesus was tempted by the devil in the wilderness, He did not question His sonship because He felt weak. When He was accused by religious leaders, He did not let their words define Him. When Satan entered Judas and Judas betrayed Jesus, He did not allow the shame to define who He was. Spiritual warfare begins to have an edge over us when we start to believe that we are anything other than God's beloved child and Christ's chosen ambassador on this earth. As Scripture reminds us in Romans 8, we are inseparable from the love of God.

Be Sure of Who God Is

When we go through enough resistance in life, our hearts can default to bad assumptions about God. *Maybe He doesn't care. Maybe He's punishing me. Maybe He likes this.* But Psalm 100:5 says, "The LORD is good, and his faithful love endures forever; his faithfulness, through all generations." Friend, the enemy would love nothing more than for you to turn on Jesus during hard times, when on the contrary, it will be your confidence in God's character and intention that will sustain you through dark valleys.

Know Your Real Enemy

Spiritual attacks have a way of distracting us from who the real enemy is. We may think it's that irrational family member and spend months obsessing about how she's the absolute worst. We may blame our church for the intense feelings of condemnation and unworthiness we feel. Yet Ephesians 6:12 says, "Our struggle is not against flesh and blood, but against the rulers, against the authorities, against the cosmic powers of this darkness, against evil, spiritual forces in the heavens."

Be Mindful of Your Thought Life

When our minds are untethered to God's truth, we become agreeable to the enemy. Whatever he wants us to think, feel, and do, we will slip into thinking, feeling, and doing without contest unless we are proactive about the thoughts we entertain. This is why it says in 2 Corinthians 10:5, "We take every thought captive to obey Christ."

Be Embedded in a Christ-Centered Community

Isolation makes us vulnerable. Do you want to be stronger in the Spirit? Involve others who are rooted in biblical truth and led by the Spirit. No one will outgrow the need for community to remain spiritually strong. Ecclesiastes 4:9–10 says, "Two are better than one because they have a good reward for their efforts. For if either falls, his companion can lift him up; but pity the one who falls without another to lift him up."

Repent Quickly and Walk in Holiness

James 4:7–8 says, "Submit to God. Resist the devil, and he will flee from you. Draw near to God, and he will draw near to you. Cleanse your hands, sinners, and purify your hearts, you double-minded." Demonic spirits are like flies, and our unrepented sins are like the trash that those flies are drawn to. Get rid of the flies by clearing away the trash. Unrepented sins point to the parts of your heart that are not yet in full submission to the Lord.

Be Wary of Bitter Roots Growing in Your Heart

I once preached for a college ministry, and our first worship service together felt like pulling teeth. There was a heaviness in the air, and the people looked dead. I knew something was off, so I gathered with the volunteer team and the pastor in charge and learned that there was a lot of bitterness in the congregation due to a turnover in leadership. The next day, I led the congregation in a time of forgiveness and letting go of blame. When we began to worship, people started to get baptized by the Holy Spirit, and new life was in the room! Ephesians 4:26–27 says, "Be angry and do not sin. Don't let the sun go down on your anger, and don't give the devil an opportunity."

EQUIPPING CHRIST'S DISCIPLES

So, how do we become the type of Christian who can heal the sick and cast out demons? If you are anything like I've been over the years, you're probably itching for me to get to the *how* of it all. You know you're anointed by the Holy Spirit. You know that the anointing gives you spiritual authority. But how do we take what we have and release God's rule and reign over this earth? How can we see Christ's order confront the demonic strongholds and evil forces around us?

Here's the thing: We cannot embody God's power. We must embody Christ Himself. Many Christians pursue Christ's power without prioritizing the pursuit of Christlikeness. We tend to imitate what we see, so if we see our church leaders or a well-known Christian influencer being used by God in a way that we admire, we can find ourselves mimicking their way of speech and personal expression. We take on their go-to phrases and their style of prayer hoping to unlock the results they have in our own lives. However, the goal is not to become an alternate or even a supposedly upgraded version of ourselves. Instead, it's to be like Jesus. Even the apostle Paul told the believing

Corinthians that if they were to imitate him, they should be imitating him as he imitates Christ.*

Anyone can covet the authority to cast out demons and the power to heal the sick. It doesn't even take a Christian to want that. Even nonbelievers can be fascinated by the supernatural and drawn to the attention that spiritual gifts garner. The desire to perform miracles can easily be fueled by ego, insecurity, or even curiosity. People may want to see the visible power of Jesus without ever really loving Him. It takes a born-again believer who has the Holy Spirit to want to submit to the Father as Jesus did. To learn how to pray like Christ. To forgive like He did. To be humble like our King. To sit with the unwanted and marginalized like Immanuel.

This is a call to true discipleship. If you've ever wanted to grow as an anointed follower of Christ or if you've ever felt the stirrings for more than mere moments of spiritual activity, then hear this clearly, Friend: Discipleship is the journey. The road to cultivating the anointing is a narrow one that will shake, break, and form you into Christlikeness. You know you are a disciple when you are growing in not just spiritual activity but also spiritual resemblance to Jesus Christ.

Remember when Jesus empowered seventy-two people to preach the gospel, heal the sick, and cast out demons in Luke 10? What's beautiful about this scene is the sequence leading up to it. Just one chapter earlier, at the beginning of Luke 9, Jesus commissioned the twelve disciples, the well-known, hand-picked group who would later be known as the apostles. Much of the rest of Luke 9 focuses on what it means to be a disciple. Take up your cross daily, deny yourself, and

* 1 Corinthians 11:1.

follow Jesus. Then, right afterward, Luke 10 begins with Jesus sending out the seventy-two. These seventy-two did not include the Twelve, and still, Jesus sent them out with His authority as well. They were able to do the exact same things as the Twelve did. They preached, healed, and cast out demons. Why? Because they, too, followed Jesus. That's the point, isn't it? It's not about trying to be the special Twelve. It's about being Christ's disciple.

Ever since we were born, we've been enculturated to believe that power is earned. Christian discipleship is a lifelong unlearning of the world's ways. Instead of climbing higher, hustling harder, and fighting for influence, we are to embrace the way of Christ and do the opposite. Lower ourselves. Sit in the least desirable place at the table. Trust God like a child. Wash feet. Share what we have without expecting anything in return. Forgive. The world crowns the strong, but God anoints His disciples.

THE METHOD: LOVE GOD AND LOVE PEOPLE

One of the toughest deliverance cases I've witnessed was a young lady whom we'll call Kate. The demonic oppression on Kate was obvious, even for a nonbeliever to see. She couldn't handle entering the church sanctuary. She came to church every weekend because her best friends regularly brought her, but she always waited outside in the lobby. Quite often, Kate told us about the demons that were in her because she heard them daily. She wanted to join us for Sunday worship, but she would always stop at the door. She liked our worship music and liked hearing about Jesus, but when anyone would try to pray for her, she would freeze and be incapable of movement or speech. No one was able to get the demons out of her. I tried the standard deliverance prayers that I've learned from other pastors, but like I said, there's wisdom in strategies, but this case required a higher level of anointing. Several other pastors tried, too, to no avail.

After a year of no progress, the hearts of Kate's church friends began to break on her behalf. It was getting harder and harder for everyone to see her remain in bondage, to remain sitting in the lobby week after week, assuming lies like God didn't want her anyway. No pastor, small group leader, volunteer, or even guest speaker was able to "fix" the situation. Her friends finally decided they wouldn't stand for it any longer. Their faith wouldn't allow them to simply let this be. So they rallied brothers and sisters of the church, probably about ten others, to begin fasting and praying for Kate. Then one evening at church, we all gathered around Kate, with her permission of course, to pray. We called out to Jesus, asking Him to free her, and commanded the enemy to leave her and never come back. Some sang God's praises and interceded in the background. After about thirty minutes, Kate, who was once always frozen when being prayed for, started weeping. Eventually, she cried out, "Save me, Jesus! I love You, Jesus!" That evening was the first time I saw her lifting her hands to worship Christ. She was free.

Kate's story reminds us that the ministry of healing and deliverance must be rooted in love. I want to mention 1 Corinthians 14:1 again, which says, "Pursue love and desire spiritual gifts." It's good to want to see bodies restored, minds renewed, and demonic oppression broken off, but it must come from our intimate connection with the Holy Spirit and our love for the people we want to help. Healing and deliverance are acts of service, not performance, and they must be fueled by our friendship with Jesus. As you approach the person who needs healing or deliverance, here are three things to remember:

1. Discern the Need and Root Cause

Every ailment has a root cause, and true healing requires us to address it. Start your time with the person you are going to pray for by asking Jesus to give both of you wisdom and insight. Then converse with the person about what they need. Does this person need a prayer for healing, or do they need the power of the Holy Spirit to choose a lifestyle change? Is this situation rooted in sin or demonic oppression? And do they need counseling? You can't know some of these answers based on what you hear and see physically. You need the Holy Spirit's guidance. Although the necessary understanding can come to you on the spot by His grace, knowing His will and hearing His voice are a fruit of your ongoing communion with Him. Furthermore, you must have honor and esteem for the person you are helping in order to discern properly as well. Some people who need healing, whether it be spiritual, mental, or physical, will not always be the sweet, grateful, and willing persons you'd hope they'd be in receiving your help. Sometimes they're jaded or defensive, and it could come off as if something is not right with them spiritually. Others may be desperately needy and require a bit of patience instead of a whole deliverance prayer. Whatever it is, if you are approaching the person you are about to serve with judgment or accusation in your heart, it will muddle your ability to properly see what they need.

2. Pray

Pray and do so out loud so that the person you're praying for can join you in agreement. Like I've said before, it's not so much about the formulaic phrases you say but, rather, about the anointing and authority in your prayers. However, be specific. Is it pain in the shoulder? Ask Jesus to take away the pain in the shoulder. Is it demonic visions and manifestations? Ask Jesus to cast it out in His name. Invite the Holy Spirit to do the work. Once you grow in your ability to pray in this way, you can also pray prayers of authority if the Spirit stirs them up in you. Prayers of authority command evil and affliction away in the name of Jesus. They can sound like, "I command you to leave in Jesus's name." They can also sound like praying for healing into someone's ailment: "In the name of Jesus, I pray healing over your leg! I command every pain to leave." As you do this, don't strive to will the enemy away by the volume of your voice. You must do all things and say all things with a deep awareness of the Holy Spirit. You may find that as you begin prayer, you need to ask further questions. Is there a bitter root in the person that requires them to go through a time of forgiveness? Is there an unrepented sin? If so, give the person an opportunity to repent, forgive, and let go of all that is keeping them from their healing and deliverance. Furthermore, whenever I pray for healing or deliverance, I prefer a third person to be present as well, for the sake of accountability and support.

3. Respond with Patience and Kindness

There are many healing and deliverance ministries out there, and not all of them are done in an edifying and encouraging manner. Because people can still operate in their spiritual gifts without growing in maturity or without their character being in line with Christ's, they may get the job done in the moment, but it could have its consequences. They may hurt the people they are trying to serve. Just because someone is being oppressed by demons doesn't mean that they themselves are demons. You cannot forget the human made in God's image that's still there. You must treat all people with dignity. The same goes for healing. Just because you don't get results right away doesn't mean you discard the person and move on to the next person right away. Sometimes the healing comes as we take our time, discern, and pray for the Holy Spirit to break through. Sometimes the healing comes later, and on occasion, the healing doesn't come in our timing. Ultimately, we do not treat people like failed projects. If your prerogative is to love and serve the person with prayer, you can always succeed in this. The Holy Spirit does the rest.

I hope this chapter has boosted your confidence in the Holy Spirit to release God's kingdom wherever you are. We must not become attached to methods but, rather, be attached to the One who does the healing and deliverance Himself. Ultimately, people have been healed by just a touch of the hand or no contact at all! I've seen deliverance happen with someone singing praises over a person. These simple principles I laid out are where you begin the journey of stewarding the anointing of the Holy Spirit in you. However, if you feel called to grow in this ministry, I encourage you to dive deeper into other resources as well.

PUT IT INTO PRACTICE

1. Where do you recognize spiritual warfare in your life? How does it manifest?
2. In what ways can you walk in spiritual authority through the spiritual warfare?
3. Whom can you pray for that needs healing (spiritual, physical, or mental)?

12

RAISE THE DEAD

My husband and I were over the moon when we discovered that I was pregnant with our third child. Having so many children in a short amount of time was not what we anticipated, but it was a welcomed gift. At that point, we were friendly with my ob-gyn, and following through with next steps was becoming second nature to us. We knew the drill: Book that first appointment, do a sonogram, and listen for a heartbeat. Being that this was my third time around, I was fairly casual about the formalities, so I went to my first appointment a few weeks later than what I'd usually done. My husband and I cheerfully greeted the ladies at the front desk and waited as the sonogram was being set up. We saw her on the screen in her tiny, fragile form . . . with no heartbeat. Although I felt my chest tighten and my stomach turn in panic, our doctor's face did not break into alarm. He calmly investigated a bit further. Then he looked on my grieving face with compassion, and being a man of faith himself, he encouraged us to pray and return to him in two weeks. I wept through the car ride home. Over the last few weeks, I had already made space for this child in my heart. My husband and I had already discussed options for names. I was already imagining different layouts for sleeping arrangements for three children. Hope deferred really does make the heart sick.

Every day following the appointment, we clung to Jesus in prayer and invited our circle of friends to pray along with us. Sometimes I didn't have anything eloquent or persuasive to ask of God. I just kept repeating, "Please, Jesus, let my child live. Let my child live," under my breath. During those two weeks until the next appointment, life still had to go on as usual. On one of those days, my husband and I took our church leadership team to our seminary to receive special training from one of our professors. We sat around a conference table as he taught us about the anointing of the Holy Spirit. When the professor began teaching on how the Holy Spirit is the river of life, it reminded me of Ezekiel 47:9: "There will be life everywhere the river goes." As he was giving this teaching, I felt a strange sensation of heat on top of my head. I looked up to see if there was a hot lamp in the ceiling. There was nothing directly above me. Then the heat spread from the top of my head, down my face, and over the rest of my body. I imagined that's what being covered in warm oil would feel like. I felt the whole of my being burn, and I looked around wondering if I was the only one. The stillness of the room was deceiving because something very intense was happening to me while I was in my chair taking notes. The professor was still teaching—very casually, might I add, but with authority. After our session was over and I walked out of the room, I immediately felt nauseous. Up until this point, I had not experienced any pregnancy symptoms, which had also been worrisome. Yet as I walked out of that conference room, I knew that the Wendy's single cheeseburger I'd had about two hours earlier was up to no good. It did not distress me, though. I took this nausea as a gift. I knew at that moment that my child would live. It was confirmed a few days later when I went back to the doctor's office and heard the robust rhythm of our baby girl's heartbeat. We named her River.

God is the source of life. The Holy Spirit is the river of life that flows within us. Life is more than breath and a pulse. One time I walked into a church that was recently devastated by the news of their lead pastor's moral failures. As I spoke with their interim pastor and volunteers, I saw the pain that arrested them. The accusations from congregants and outsiders were draining them of their energy to its very last drop. I was there to bring a word of encouragement, but when worship began, I got nervous because the room felt dead. No matter how upbeat the music was and how hard the praise leaders tried to pick up the mood, blank faces remained. The heartbeat of this congregation was slowing down, and it was palpable even for a guest like me. I remember crying out repeatedly, "Breathe upon us, Lord!" As the worship service progressed, the Holy Spirit did indeed breathe on us—so faithfully and gently. Slowly, hands began to rise amid a chorus of hallelujahs, as weary believers were reminded of His worth. By the end of the night, the altar was flooded with those who were laying down their bitterness and disappointment at the feet of Jesus. Some wept as they forgave. Others repented. Many walked out at the end with resurrected faith, hope, and love.

His presence *is* resurrection power. When Lazarus was dead for four days, Martha said to Jesus, "I know that he will rise again in the resurrection at the last day."* To her, the resurrection was an event. Her understanding at that point was that death will one day be defeated, and whatever hope she had left was hanging on the potential of that "one day." What she believed wasn't wrong at all, but Jesus wanted to challenge her faith with a deeper revelation. Jesus wanted her to see, "I am the resurrection and the life."† The source of life was right before her. The resurrection was dependent on Him. Everything she needed for hope was in Him, not "one day."

I do not want us to deny the reality of death but to assume our God-given victory over it. Ultimately, as long as we are on this side of eternity, there will be death. Although Jesus resurrected the dead, He never denied death's inevitability while on this side of eternity. There are several resurrections throughout Scripture, including Christ's own, but that doesn't mean that every death is meant for a physical resurrection on the spot. We don't see chapters of Jesus going around and undoing the end of every deceased person He encounters. Until Jesus returns to us, everyone will die at some point. Even so, no believer is under the mastery of Death's dominion, which can show itself in many forms: separation from God, soul decay, body decay, corruption, injustice, oppression, futility.

UNDERSTANDING DEATH

Everyone is immortal. When you're with people, pause and look around. Every single person you see will spend eternity either with God or without God—an eternity in heavenly glory

* John 11:24.
† John 11:25.

or an eternity of torment. Physical death isn't an end; it's a doorway to forever. To understand God's resurrection power, we must understand what death really means in the Bible.

Let's revisit the beginning again because it is the blueprint to understanding what God intended and how we got here. The Garden of Eden was a paradise of abundant life. Every plant, animal, and person thrived by the Creator's breath. It was this way because the presence of God was at the center of this garden and humans lived in harmony with His will and way. At the center of this garden was the tree of the knowledge of good and evil, and with it was the choice to keep this relationship intact. If they ate from it, God said that on that very day, they would certainly die.* If you know how the rest of the story goes, you know that Adam and Eve did eat the fruit from this tree and that they continued the rest of their lives outside of the garden. Did God change His mind, or did He lie about the certainty of death? Neither, because death is not just about physical termination here on earth. When Adam and Eve disrupted their communion with God by disobedience, they experienced a spiritual death, which was consequently a separation from their life-giver.

If we separate a baby from his mother's arms and leave him isolated in the wilderness, we would assume that undoubtedly means death for the baby. Why? Because for a baby, a parent is a source of life. Sustenance and protection come from a parent. Guidance and a sense of identity come from the parent. Even if, by the slightest of chances, the baby physically survives the isolation, how would he know who he is and how to live as he is

* Genesis 2:17.

meant to? In that same way, separation from the Creator also meant death for Adam and Eve.

That act of disobedience in Eden created a spiritual rupture that opened the door to death's effects. This allowed the flood of decay to enter the earth and infect our existence. Adam and Eve were cut off from the life-giving presence of God, so as they walked away from the garden, death's fingerprints began to show. Now our bodies are prone to illness. Relationships rupture with hatred. The mind produces murderous and lustful thoughts. From that moment forward, the human story became entangled with suffering and corruption. By going our own way, we submitted this world and our bodies to the enemy's order. Because of our rebellion, Death was given license to ravage our existence with anxiety. Death was given permission to riddle our thoughts with inferiority and self-condemnation. Death was able to break families with violence and corrupt neighborhoods with greed. Until Jesus.

Romans 5:17 says, "If by the one man's trespass, death reigned through that one man, how much more will those who receive the overflow of grace and the gift of righteousness reign in life through the one man, Jesus Christ." His blood shed and body broken was heaven's remedy. His resurrection brought about our complete reconciliation with our Creator. We are no longer cursed by death because we are filled with life. We are no longer strangers and enemies of God but have been made His children by the Holy Spirit. In achieving this, Jesus robbed Death of its rights over you. You are now re-plugged into the outlet of life. The power of the Holy Spirit runs through your veins once again. You may still feel the lure of temptation and the sting of fear, but you are no longer their slave. Shame cannot claim you. Condemnation cannot trap you into hiding any longer.

When Jesus says that He is the resurrection, that means you carry the resurrection power of the Holy Spirit with you as well. Wherever you go, you bring life. Just as my seminary professor released the power of life over me while teaching God's words, you can release the power of life over your schools, your homes, and your neighborhoods. You don't just carry information about God. You carry the Holy Spirit that resurrects the hopeless, the ashamed, the fearful, and the lost.

THE WAR OF HOPE

Sometimes a loved one succumbs to cancer. Other times, an unforeseen incident takes a parent or a spouse. A friend may have lost everything because of the destructive consequences of addiction. A believer may have turned away from God because the memories of abuse still flood their mind. To be an anointed Christian who believes that the resurrection power of the Holy Spirit gives life is a clashing confrontation to this dying world. What does it mean to resurrect dead people and dead places by the power of the Holy Spirit? Does the Holy Spirit still have command in funeral homes and grieving rooms?

There is a tension that comes with the power we carry. We sit with someone in hospice, and yet we're still commissioned to speak life. After years of counseling and hard work, a marriage falls apart, and yet we still believe in the power of forgiveness. We walk into a church broken apart by divisive pride, and yet we are to believe that it's still the beloved bride of Christ. How can we bring life to the things that are already dead? How do we revive what looks beyond saving?

Hopelessness is one of the by-products of death because death is the ultimate disappointment. We as humans were designed by a perfect and holy God. We were made for fruitfulness. We were created to thrive. We were created to live forever. So, when the world deals its blows and what we prayed for doesn't happen, disappointment is a visceral shock. I'm sure Mary and Martha knew this full well. If only Jesus had come in time! If only Jesus had left for Bethany when Lazarus's sisters sent the SOS message to Him.

They must have sent that message to Jesus while straining for hope. Mary and Martha, by that point, knew that death wasn't necessary and healing was always an option with God. Yet Jesus did not respond as they had hoped. They watched their brother draw his last breath. In Jewish tradition, it was believed that the spirit of a person hovered over the body for three days hoping to reenter it. Perhaps there was the tiniest part of them that felt like maybe, just maybe, he wasn't really dead, at least in those three days. Maybe if Jesus came within those days, there would be hope. But He didn't. He came on the fourth day. You can imagine, then, the ache that must have been in Mary's voice when she cried out, "Lord, if you had been here, my brother wouldn't have died!"*

There's a sense of despairing finality to a death, and it's not always a physical death that arouses it. It could be the death of a marriage. The death of a career. The death of a season of our life. The death of our goals and dreams. The death of a friendship. The death of a church. We could have tried to make it work. We could have done everything to make a way. We could have fasted, practically begged God, to keep it living on. And

* John 11:32.

yet all we're left with is fragments and memories of what was. We may even be tempted to think, *Who cares if I'm an anointed Christian at this point?*

Disappointment will do that. It will poison your heart with hopelessness. It incessantly whispers that your faith didn't work, that maybe the anointing on your life is wishful thinking. Friend, let me tell you this: That's exactly what the enemy wants. He wants to use death, in all its forms, to paralyze you with hopelessness. But whether you feel it or not, whether you're doing great as a Christian or not, Christ's resurrection power is still in you, and it doesn't deny that something has died. Instead, it declares that Death doesn't get the final word. The shame you feel doesn't negate His presence. The fear that's racing through your mind cannot overpower the Holy Spirit. The anointing doesn't disappear in the ruins. It's still in the works.

The most faithful thing Mary and Martha did was to bring Jesus to their greatest disappointment, to the place of their darkest despair. They could have deserted Him out of bitterness. They could have disregarded His words when He told them to open the tomb, despite the chances that it would release the toxic stench of a decaying corpse. But they stuck by Him. This was how they fought their battle of hope. They stuck with Jesus.

Jairus did the same thing. He ran to Jesus with this plea: "My little daughter is dying. Come and lay your hands on her so that she can get well and live."* But as Jesus went with him toward his house, a woman in need interrupted. It was a bleeding woman who touched Jesus's clothing and was completely healed.

* Mark 5:23.

Jesus stopped for this. The crowd stood around them in awe. I'm sure as this was happening, Jairus must have felt the angst of needing to return home to his daughter in time. Her belabored breathing and wilting body must have been seared in his mind as Jesus seemed to take His time speaking to others. Imagine what he must have felt when people came from his home and told him it was too late. "Your daughter is dead. Why bother the teacher anymore?"*

Why bother Him anymore? Why pray anymore? Why believe anymore? Why praise anymore? Why love Him anymore? Because no matter the circumstance, Jesus is the resurrection. Like Mary and Martha, Jairus held on to Jesus and brought Him to his place of greatest despair. And he got to witness Christ's resurrection power unfold—not according to his plans but for God's glory.

Stewarding the resurrection power that is within you doesn't mean you won't be disappointed. It doesn't mean you must feel powerful after crushed expectations. You release this power by warring for hope amid despair. Bring Jesus to that estranged relationship and follow His voice. Bring Jesus to your infertility and child loss and cry with Him. As long as the resurrection and life is with you, Death cannot have the final word. May you feel the words of Paul as a prayer over you: "[May you] understand the incredible greatness of God's power for us who believe him. This is the same mighty power that raised Christ from the dead and seated him in the place of honor at God's right hand in the heavenly realms."†

* Mark 5:35.

† Ephesians 1:19–20, NLT.

DIE TO LIVE

Just because an anointed believer carries resurrection power doesn't mean they are automatically abounding with life. Remember how a Holy Spirit carrier isn't always someone who is living by the filling of the Holy Spirit? To release life to others, we must know how, according to Scripture, to steward and not quench it. If we live in accordance with the Holy Spirit, we will abound in divine life. If we live quenching and grieving the Holy Spirit, our flesh may feel a temporary gratification, but we would be living in accordance with the old order that Jesus already died for, the one that is separated from the living power of God. Are there areas in your life where you must die to yourself so that you may live in the fullness of God's resurrection power?

Sin

James 1:15 says, "After desire has conceived, it gives birth to sin, and when sin is fully grown, it gives birth to death." There are sins that seem acceptable and are even embraced in today's secular culture, such as idolatry, selfish ambition, and lust. However, be mindful of what God has deemed counter to His will and ways.

Refusing to Accept Grace

When we attempt to earn forgiveness and favor instead of embracing God's grace, we fall into the trap of legalism. Second Corinthians 3:6 says, "The letter kills, but the Spirit gives life." If we have difficulty accepting God's grace, we are allowing Death to take hold of our life with shame and condemnation. If we want the benefits of salvation, we must agree with what

Jesus did to reconcile us with the Father. We must receive His forgiveness and mercy.

An Ungoverned Mind

Why is it that some of us come out of Sunday service feeling the peace and joy of the Spirit but spend Monday through Saturday in anxiety and unrest? Oftentimes, it's because our minds refuse to bend to the Holy Spirit's truth. Romans 8:6 says, "The mindset of the flesh is death, but the mindset of the Spirit is life and peace."

Evil Speech

We may believe we are a child of God, but we may say things like "I'm good for nothing" or "I'm done for!"—consequently using words that align with death and not life. This can be true in how we speak to others as well. We may love our friend or family member, but if our words to them constantly sound like "You are never going to change!" then we are not speaking life into them. Instead, our words are in agreement with death! Proverbs 18:21 says, "Death and life are in the power of the tongue."

Ignoring Wisdom

Biblical wisdom will keep us from aligning with Death. We could have all the love for Jesus we want and still bring damage and wreckage to our lives if we ignore sound, God-given wisdom. Proverbs 8:36 says of wisdom, "The one who misses me harms himself; all who hate me love death."

Pride

Although God redeems all things, He doesn't redeem pride. He simply rids us of pride. We either choose pride or choose life. A gifted Christian will not bring life to anyone if they are also carrying pride. Proverbs 16:18 says, "Pride comes before destruction."

A practical picture of how to live with God's resurrection power on full display in our lives is the apostle Paul's times in prison. It would be easy to assume that when he was unjustly bound, it would be the death of his evangelistic ministry. The death of his hopes and dreams on earth. Even so, the spiritually dead came to life where Paul was trapped! Prisoners and prison guards came to know Jesus every time Paul was imprisoned. Chains could not imprison the resurrection power of the Holy Spirit in Paul! Even when we read the brief four-chapter book of Philippians, which is one of Paul's epistles from prison, the word *joy* (or renditions of it) is mentioned sixteen times.* He was around death, but death could not take hold of his mind and heart. And while he was there, his words were, "My goal is to know him and the power of his resurrection and the fellowship of his sufferings, being conformed to his death."† He could have said "I want a better prison cell" or "I want my rights back." He could have fought to live the way he wanted to, but he knew that he already had the source of true life with him. Instead, Paul wanted an experiential, intimate knowledge of Jesus, along with His power and suffering. This requires more than Sunday mornings; it calls for your entire life.

* Bob Roane, "Joyful Life in Christ: Overview of Philippians," *Words of Hope* (blog), September 23, 2024, https://wohbm.org/joyful-life-in-christ-overview-of-philippians.

† Philippians 3:10.

PUT IT INTO PRACTICE

1. In what way have you experienced a death (physical, spiritual, relational)? How were you able to experience life even through that death? Or how are you working it out now?
2. Where have you lived in agreement with Death? What can you repent of?
3. In what situation can you believe and pray for life, for you or others?

13

PREACH THE GOSPEL

My husband's grandmother was a treasure trove of tales, and every visit with her was blessed with the same stories, again and again. How Jesus healed her husband of stomach cancer. How God protected them during the Korean War. How Jesus had blessed her immeasurably since she'd given her life to Him. Being that she was an elderly woman in northern New Jersey who did not speak English or know the culture of her new land, most of her days were spent in prayer at home. The pages of her Bible were tissue-thin, worn soft by years of turning and tears. Her knees were calloused and swollen as a witness to the countless hours of prayer spent on them. She never received an education or knew much about the world beyond her home. However, she knew Jesus—intimately, authentically, and passionately.

On one of our visits, she approached me slyly and tried to sneak a hundred-dollar bill in my pocket. She whispered in my ear, "I know I'm going to meet Jesus soon. But I don't want to be ashamed to see Him because I couldn't do much with my life. Use this money to purchase Bibles for North Koreans who don't know our Jesus yet." With my broken Korean and her broken English, I tried to gently explain that it's not as simple as putting a hundred dollars to it. However, I felt her heart and intention that day, and I believe the Lord was honored by it. She wanted to use her life, in whatever way possible, for others to know Jesus, and she wanted to take advantage of the time she had left to do so. Like many Christians, she felt limited in her ability to share the good news because she wasn't a pastor or preacher.

My grandmother-in-law passed away about three years later, and I am positive that she would not have been ashamed to show Jesus the fruit of her life. It was clear to those who were left behind—including all sixty of the children, grandchildren, and great-grandchildren who were also Christ followers and servants of the gospel due to her faithful years of pouring out her testimony and prayers. Her life is proof that our lives can be anointed to bring people to Christ, even if we never hold a microphone at a pulpit.

NO OTHER EVANGELIST LIKE YOU

You are called to be an evangelist. Yes, you! The term *evangelist* means slightly different things to different Christians, depending on their church traditions. For some, it's a title for a gifted preacher who can bring the house down with a forty-minute sermon and convince that stubborn friend of theirs to walk up to the altar. For others, it's a street evangelist who holds signs and hands out tracts. Maybe it's a missionary in a different country. More often than not, Christians tend to disassociate themselves from evangelism because they do not feel as though it's their particular strength or spiritual gift. Or they may have seen it done poorly, so they may not feel as if it's for them. Most Christians do want to see the people around them saved; they just don't know how because they are not a master preacher or a well-versed apologist.

Before Jesus ascended from earth, He made the commission for every disciple clear: "Go, therefore, and make disciples of all nations, baptizing them in the name of the Father and of the Son and of the Holy Spirit, teaching them to observe everything I have commanded you."* How can believers fit evangelism into their everyday lives? How can we win souls for Christ without being inauthentic to how the Lord has uniquely designed us? First, let's clarify this commission that He's given every believer. What are we to make? It doesn't say go and make church attendees or go and make more supporters of your political beliefs. It also doesn't say go and make people who will have spiritual experiences at church while refusing to submit their lives to God. The assignment is to make disciples who accept Christ's grace and have submitted to His lordship. So it is not just about preaching sermons.

The Great Commission isn't reserved for special people who have a knack for public speaking. Preaching is a part of evangelism, but it isn't the whole of it. Yes, Jesus preached, but He also ate with social pariahs and moral failures. He had a conversation with a woman at a well. He took notice of the marginalized. He fed people. He wept with people. The Great Commission does not require a social media following and a

* Matthew 28:19–20.

platform. We can be misunderstood and overlooked and still usher people toward eternity with God.

The only requirement for evangelism is the anointing of the Holy Spirit. In Acts 1:8, Jesus said, "You will receive power when the Holy Spirit has come on you, and you will be my witnesses in Jerusalem, in all Judea and Samaria, and to the ends of the earth." In other words, the anointing will qualify you to be a witness.

Every chapter that we've spent together has been about the work of the Holy Spirit's presence and power. As you walk with the Holy Spirit and practice His presence and power, you will not be of this world. You will be an alien in your family. You will be "other" in your town. Trust me, people will notice that there's an air of difference to you. Sometimes when I walk through New York City, random strangers will say, "Your energy is different!" To which I smile because I know that the "different energy" is actually the Holy Spirit.

Being authentically and unapologetically anointed is what will make you the evangelist the Lord has called you to be. These last twelve chapters have explored ways you can uniquely employ the anointing of God. You may not be a raging extrovert, but the Holy Spirit may use you mightily when you are helpful to your neighbors. You may not have an impressive following on social media, but you can still cook a mean casserole and open your home to welcome strangers. This is not some optimistic spin to coddle your self-esteem and do your little part in this world. Friend, you must know this: There is no one on this earth who has the capacity to reach everyone on this earth. There is no church on this earth, no matter how big and influential, that can reach every single soul on its own. God bless the small and midsize churches because they have a reach unlike any other ministry. God bless the Bible studies in the lunchrooms at work. There are people within *your* reach—and you may be the only Christian who can access them! If you are a single young adult, there are some people only you can reach with the gospel. If you are a high schooler, there are some students only you can speak into! If you are a senior citizen in an adult daycare, there is a soul sitting in the corner of the activity room that only you can love to life.

In that same way, there was no one who could have reached my husband's family like my grandmother-in-law did. She didn't have a car, an education, or any sort of societal influence. However, she had the anointing of the Holy Spirit. She prophesied over her children and grandchildren at every visitation. She served hot meals. She would intercede in prayer day and night. She "preached" on the living room couch to only one or two people at a time, and she didn't have to include a pristine intro, biblical exegesis, or illustrations. She didn't have a worship team backing her up. She preached with her life stories. She was a witness to the work of Jesus Christ in her life, during the Korean War, and through the uncertain journey of immigration. And although she is now at home with the Lord, her life is still ministering to many of us today.

BE GOOD NEWS

Evangelism can feel heavy, especially in places where any mention of Jesus is discouraged or forbidden. Maybe you're trying to share the gospel with someone whose faith in their religion has been shaped since childhood, and to them, embracing Jesus might feel like losing everything they've ever known. That is no small task, Friend. You have been given a sacred calling.

In Christian communities, especially in the West, there's often a lot of talk about calling. It sounds like "What career should I pursue?" or "What's my unique destiny?" While your specific missional assignment can shift with seasons, one of your callings never changes: You are called to be a witness of Jesus Christ. This begins when you become a believer and lasts until your final breath. It may not look like testifying on a stage or in front of a camera. It could look like loving difficult people, having the courage to speak the truth, or endlessly praying. But make no mistake, being a witness is the most honorable assignment you will carry in this life.

The Holy Spirit will help you. If there's anyone who understood the weight of evangelizing through roadblocks and challenges, it is Brother Yun, also affectionately nicknamed The Heavenly Man. He is known for his miraculous faith journey while being a persecuted Christian in China, and many of his evangelistic stories were behind bars. One of those stories was about a murderer named Huang, who was so violent and suicidal that everyone in the prison considered him to be a demonic animal. But when Huang was placed in Brother Yun's prison cell, Brother Yun encouraged his cellmates to treat the man as if he were Jesus Himself. Because Huang was used to being treated like a soulless beast in this prison, he was shocked by the gentle compassion lavished on him the moment he entered the cell. His new cellmates shared their rationed water. They helped disinfect his wounds. A turning point arose when the prisoners received their weekly mantou, a steamed bun. Brother Yun felt stirred by the Holy Spirit to save a portion of his mantou for Huang, although he himself was desperately starving. During Huang's next outburst the following day, Brother Yun felt a nudge from the Holy Spirit to give him the mantou. This undeserved kindness reached a seemingly unreachable soul, and Huang broke down in tears. He said, "Older brother, why do you love me like this? Why didn't you eat your bread last night? I am a murderer, hated by all men."* It was then that Brother Yun shared the gospel with Huang, and Huang accepted his personal invitation to be a part of God's family that day.

Jesus had a mission to seek and save the lost. Preaching with divine wisdom was only a fraction of what He did to accomplish this on earth. He taught the good news, but He also *was* good news. How? He met people in their areas of need. People needed healing, so He healed them. People needed freedom, so He delivered them from demons. He fed the hungry. He restored dignity to the desperate. Jesus demonstrated that evangelism isn't solely accomplished by getting people to believe what we think. It's choosing to show up in people's needs. Remember, the enemy has come to steal, kill, and destroy.† Those who have yet to know Jesus have an unfulfilled need that can be met only by God. An evangelist finds that need and honors it. After all, Jesus didn't look at the hungry crowd and tell them to go feed themselves and then come back to listen to His important message. He met them in their hunger. He didn't wait for the woman caught in adultery to change her behavior before He stood up to protect her. He met her in her shame. The most Christlike thing you can do where you are is to take note of the needs around you in your unique context and meet people there with the anointing in your life.

* Brother Yun and Paul Hattaway, *The Heavenly Man: The Remarkable True Story of Chinese Christian Brother Yun* (Hendrickson, 2009), 129.

† John 10:10.

People in my life may not be physically hungry and they tend to have enough resources if ever injured or ill, but they still have one pressing need they cannot meet on their own: peace. I cannot tell you how many people come to our church because they are tired of being paralyzed with anxiety. Some of the most powerful conversations I've had with nonbelievers in my neighborhood have been about their worries and fears. Their pathway to Jesus is the realization that peace of mind comes from God. And when they seek Him, Jesus meets them in their need with His presence.

DIVINE APPOINTMENTS

For evangelism to be a lifestyle and not just a special event, we need to know how to recognize God's divine appointments for us. Divine appointments are when the Holy Spirit orchestrates redemptive moments and encounters with people. The book of Acts is full of divine appointments. Philip was led by the Holy Spirit to help an Ethiopian eunuch understand Scripture and get baptized by the side of the road.* Peter received a vision to go see Cornelius, a Gentile centurion, in his home, marking a pivotal moment for the church's outreach to the Gentiles.† Although Paul wanted to preach in Asia, the Holy Spirit diverted him to Macedonia, where he happened upon a woman by the river who heard him preach the gospel and became the first European convert.‡ Jesus also recognized divine appointments. Whether it was finding Zacchaeus in a tree or a Samaritan

* Acts 8:26–40.

† Acts 10.

‡ Acts 16:11–15.

woman by the well, Jesus, too, took time to pause what He was doing to stop for one person in need of the good news.

So, what can we learn from the example of the early church, and how can we recognize divine appointments today?

1. *Make space for the Holy Spirit's directions.* Philip, Peter, and Paul happened to be at the right place at the right time because they were intentionally listening to the Holy Spirit's directions. Before a full day of ministry, Jesus often started with prayer, receiving His marching orders from His Father before deciding on the course of the day. Does your life have space for the Holy Spirit to give you a mission?
2. *Be interruptible for Jesus.* Notice how many of these divine appointments were unexpected. Paul tried to stay on task for evangelism in Asia, but the Spirit kept him from proceeding. Paul's agenda was interrupted so that he could meet Lydia in Philippi of Macedonia. Jesus was on His way to Galilee, but He had to go to Samaria first to sit with the Samaritan woman. Is your life in too much of a hurry to have room for God to interrupt you?
3. *Leave your comfort zone.* Peter took a risk to go to Cornelius's home because Cornelius was a Gentile. The Jewish people were traditionally forbidden to associate with or enter the homes of Gentiles. I'm sure it was also uncomfortable for Paul to reroute to Macedonia. Sometimes Jesus will challenge us to leave our bubbles of comfort or our well-curated plans to reach someone. Are you willing to go where He leads, even if it's uncomfortable?

4. *Don't be afraid of what to say.* The goal of recognizing and following through on divine assignments is simply to show up where the Holy Spirit leads. We do this while also trusting that the Holy Spirit will give us the words to say, if such words are needed. Jesus said to His disciples, "Don't worry beforehand what you will say, but say whatever is given to you at that time, for it isn't you speaking, but the Holy Spirit."* Are you trusting that the Holy Spirit will give you the words to say, and are you listening for them?

After moving to a new area, I started looking for a new hairstylist for my haircuts and color. Since we are a ministering family, I wanted a salon within a specific budget. While googling options, I felt the Holy Spirit highlight a particular salon, but it was the sort that social media influencers and models would go to. Immediately, I swiped past, thinking, *No way.* However, my eyes kept returning to the name of the salon, and I asked the Holy Spirit, "Are You trying to tell me something here?" I felt Him say, *Go there. I have people I want you to meet.*

"But Lord!" I complained. "I can't afford this place!"

Go there.

For a few days, I questioned whether I was hearing things wrong. It just felt completely out of place for me to go to this salon. I was thinking about me, my comfort zone, and my budget. The next day, a friend electronically wired me money as a gift because she felt led to be generous that day. It was the exact amount for the hair session. But still, in my stubbornness, I told the Lord, "I can't in my right mind use this money for my

* Mark 13:11.

hair. If you tell my husband that this money is for my hair, then I'll go!" Thank God He is gracious and kind.

The next day, Dave and I were praying with a family friend. We were sitting in a circle, listening to the Holy Spirit and prophesying. My husband looked confused as he had his eyes closed. Our friend implored, "What's going on, Dave? What is God telling you?" My husband opened his eyes and said, "I don't know why, but God told me that I need to send my wife to go get her hair done!" I froze in amazement. I then told him about my friend's gift, and my stubborn self finally made that reservation. The day before my appointment, I realized I would have to pay for garage parking, which was a lot for that area. I thought, *Lord, I can't go! I don't want to waste money!* Immediately, I felt the Holy Spirit admonish me: *Faith, did I not tell you? There are people I want you to meet. You are getting caught up with secondary matters. I am leading you to what matters to* Me*!* I was amazed when a different friend (I have generous friends, apparently!) wired me money later that day, and it was the exact amount to pay for the garage parking! I stopped fighting it then. I became filled with the fear of the Holy Spirit.

I interceded the entire way to this salon, not knowing whom or what to expect. I knew by this point that Jesus just wanted me to show up. Once I settled into my salon chair, I met her. It didn't take more than five minutes for me to know that she had a deep hatred for Christians and the church. I hadn't told her that I was a pastor and a preacher for Jesus, but she went off about how narrow-minded, hypocritical Christians were ruining society. I felt her anger, but I was also filled with compassion. Being that I hadn't been to a salon in quite some time, the appointment took two hours. For two hours, I sat with her. I listened to her. When the Holy Spirit gave me words, I would encourage her. Toward the end of my appointment, she cheerfully asked, "Oh! I haven't asked you yet. What do you do?" I told her, "I'm a pastor. My husband and I lead a church." She silently continued brushing through my hair and replied, "Oh! Cool." I chuckle as I write this because this was the beginning of a beautiful friendship. For years after, she listened to my sermon clips and read my online articles. I got to encourage other workers there as well, one who even visited our church and encountered the Holy Spirit. When I look back at that season, I am humbled because who am I to determine when Jesus wants to reach someone? He gives us the Holy Spirit because He wants our participation in His redemptive story—even if it is through our hair care.

PUT IT INTO PRACTICE

1. Who are the nonbelievers around you, and in what ways can you meet them in their needs?
2. How have you made your life interruptible for the gospel? If you don't think it is, what can you do today to make space for the Holy Spirit to interrupt your plans?
3. Whom is the Holy Spirit prompting you to share your testimony with?

CONCLUSION

It's one thing to love the Holy Spirit and depend on Him. But we experience Him at another level when we begin to *move* with Him. For example, I'm a mother of four growing children, and when they were little, taking them anywhere was an Olympic-level obstacle course. Here were these four beautiful babies whom I love and who love me back. They needed me and they knew it. They clung to me because their lives depended on it. But that doesn't mean I was free to take them wherever I wanted! Just going to Target was a challenge! If I wanted to grab one item in the aisle, I had to coax one of them to stay put in the shopping cart. I had to stop another from trying to wander off. One would be mad at a sibling, and we'd have to pause to make it right. Even the simple act of grabbing an item off the shelf was limited because my children needed to grow in maturity—not just to love me but to know my will and way. Now that they've grown, there's more we can do together. We can watch movies and share our thoughts about deeper topics. We can decide together what to eat. And when we go to Target, it's now a group collaboration. We can get more done because they'll follow me wherever I go.

This is what I mean when I say there's more for you. My first published book, *Experiencing Friendship with God,* is about how the gift of the gospel is our friendship with Jesus. The purpose of your life is to know Him—intimately, authentically, and passionately. Once getting to know Him, you will undoubtedly discover that you have befriended a mover and shaker. The Holy Spirit is always up to some redemptive mischief, and He likes to take His friends along with Him.

I'm not a nature gal by any means. I love nature behind glass while I'm comfortably in an air-conditioned space. However, some of my closest friends are nature lovers. So, what have I done from time to time in the past few years? Hike. I've climbed mountains. I've walked along nature trails. My friendship with these women has taken me places I never imagined going on my own. Your friendship with Jesus will do the same.

The question is this: Will you move with the Holy Spirit? Your intimacy with Him will take you places that need a knowledge of His presence as well. Sitting with the Holy Spirit will always lead to being sent by Him too. And yes, Jesus wants this. He once said to His disciples, "The harvest is abundant, but the workers are few. Therefore, pray to the Lord of the harvest to send out workers into his harvest."* God wants our participation.

The workers are few. Jesus wants more intercessors willing to sit with the elderly at senior homes and pray for their salvation. He wants more people shepherding children to His presence. He wants more people prophesying truth to the powers

* Matthew 9:37–38.

that be in society. He wants those with spiritual gifts to pay attention to the lost and lonely on the street. To hope in places where the preaching of the gospel has been systemically forbidden. To be interruptible and available at grocery stores, hair salons, and hospitals. Who is willing to see what He sees? To say what He wants to say? To be the hands and feet of Jesus? There is no shortage of need. There's just a shortage of Holy Spirit–carrying believers who are willing to move with Him. Jesus looked at His own disciples and told them to pray for God to multiply their little army so that even today we can harvest many souls before the trumpets sound.

I once attended a Giants versus Cowboys football game for my husband's birthday. I'll be the first to admit that I'm not a big football fan, but I was there to support my husband. I went into this game with zero expectations. I even brought a Kindle with me in case I was bored! During the game, I sat in my seat, quietly minding my own business, even though I was surrounded by a wall of fans screaming, cheering, and pumping their fists. I heard roar after roar, but because the game seemed irrelevant to me, I perused social media instead. It wasn't until I started to see new notifications pop up on my phone that I began to wake from my apathy. There were headlines about some historic, once-in-a-lifetime NFL catch. It was the Giants' Odell Beckham Jr.'s one-handed touchdown catch against . . . the Cowboys. It had happened right in front of me, and I completely missed it! People still talk about that catch to this day. After the game, my husband was over the moon and couldn't believe that he was physically in the stadium for this event. I was, too, but I couldn't really say that I was actually *there.* I was completely checked out because I had no expectation. I didn't think there would be anything noteworthy to see!

Christians can behave like this too. Many are checked out from kingdom work because there is no divine expectation for what Jesus can do through them. Many believers who have the anointing of the Holy Spirit wake up each day assuming that the kingdom work doesn't include them, perhaps isn't even relevant to them. If we have no hope that the Holy Spirit has a history-making play in the works, we will be checked out with our faces buried in our Kindles and social media apps, just like I was in that stadium.

However, one day, the trumpets *will* sound. Jesus *will* return, and we *will* get to see everything that He's done on earth during humanity's time. Some may wonder, *Where was I when that was happening?* The sobering truth is that many were present but not participating. They were indwelled with the Holy Spirit and yet lived as if their lives had no part in God's unfolding story. This is meant not to stir shame but to awaken urgency.

The King is still on mission. The Spirit in you has the power. You are anointed. Do you see the harvest?

ACKNOWLEDGMENTS

I am unworthy to write this book. I say this not in self-deprecation but as a confession. Every word required strength and guidance from Jesus because I wrote about His power during one of the weakest times of my life. It is not lost on me how sacred this topic of God's anointing is. It's been nothing short of an honor to be able to dedicate the last two years exploring its mysteries. Wonderful Holy Spirit, I really hope You like this one.

To my husband, Dave: Every time I felt incapable of finishing this book, you encouraged me. You prayed when I could not pray. You believed when I could not believe. You watched the kids when I had deadlines to meet. You made me coffee when the hours were late. You helped me process my ideas during car rides. Your gift of faith has taken us on some wild and miraculous journeys, and I'm forever grateful.

To Moriah, Elias, River, and Adalynn: Being your mother

has taught me more about the anointing than anything else. I love you more—always.

To Aubrey Sampson, my weekly prayer partner and cherished friend: You prayed for me through every step of writing this book. Because of you, I had the courage to laugh through my weaknesses and remain faithful to the call.

To all the revivalists and theologians, both well known and unknown, who have gone before me to remind the church of our need for the anointing: Your lives, ministries, and words have been a lighthouse for me when I felt as though the Spirit's presence and power were too mystical for me to grasp. I know that I stand on your shoulders.

To Tom Dean: Thank you for being a constant champion to me and my family. Your Spirit-filled wisdom and help have allowed this message to become a book. What an adventure it's been!

To Jamie Lapeyrolerie and the WaterBrook team: Thank you for your constant support and enthusiasm. I've had a lot to learn, and I had to learn it fast. You made this possible, and it's been such a pleasure.

To Jesus Christ, my Lord and Savior: You are the reason I live. May every word magnify Your name!

ABOUT THE AUTHOR

FAITH EURY CHO has been a gospel preacher since she was nineteen years old and has devoted her life to helping people know and delight in the presence of God. Today she serves as a pastor, speaker, and author. She holds a master of divinity from Liberty University. Alongside her husband, Pastor David Cho, she planted and co-leads Mosaic Covenant Church in Paramus, New Jersey. Together, they enjoy raising their four children: Moriah, Elias, River, and Adalynn.

ABOUT THE TYPE

This book was set in Caledonia, a typeface designed in 1939 by W. A. Dwiggins (1880–1956) for the Merganthaler Linotype Company. Its name is the ancient Roman term for Scotland because the face was intended to have a Scottish-Roman flavor. Caledonia is considered to be a well-proportioned, businesslike face with little contrast between its thick and thin lines.